The Manager's
Book of Checklists

PEARSON
Prentice Hall
BUSINESS

Books that make you better

Books that make you better – that make you *be* better, *do* better, *feel* better. Whether you want to upgrade your personal skills or change your job, whether you want to improve your managerial style, become a more powerful communicator, or be stimulated and inspired as you work.

Prentice Hall Business is leading the field with a new breed of skills, careers and development books. Books that are a cut above the mainstream – in topic, content and delivery – with an edge and verve that will make you better, with less effort.

Books that are as sharp and smart as you are.

Prentice Hall Business.
We work harder – so you don't have to.

For more details on products, and to contact us, visit
www.pearsoned.co.uk

DEREK ROWNTREE

The Manager's Book of Checklists

Everything you need to know,
when you need to know it

3rd Edition

Harlow, England • London • New York • Boston • San Francisco • Toronto
Sydney • Tokyo • Singapore • Hong Kong • Seoul • Taipei • New Delhi
Cape Town • Madrid • Mexico City • Amsterdam • Munich • Paris • Milan

PEARSON EDUCATION LIMITED

Edinburgh Gate
Harlow CM20 2JE
Tel: +44 (0)1279 623623
Fax: +44 (0)1279 431059
Website: www.pearsoned.co.uk

First published 1996
Second edition 2000
Third edition published in Great Britain 2006

© Derek Rowntree 1996, 2006

The right of Derek Rowntree to be identified as author of this work has been asserted
by him in accordance with the Copyright, Designs and Patents Act 1988.

ISBN-13: 978-0-273-70701-1
ISBN-10: 0-273-70701-9

British Library Cataloguing in Publication Data
A catalogue record for this book is available from the British Library

Library of Congress Cataloging-in-Publication Data
Rowntree, Derek.
    The manager's book of checklists : everything you need to know, when you
need to know it / Derek Rowntree.—3rd ed.
        p. cm.
    ISBN-13: 978-0-273-70701-1 (alk. paper)
    ISBN-10: 0-273-70701-9 (alk. paper)
    1. Management. I. Title.

    HD31.R7778 2005
        658.4—dc22

                                                                        2005054674

10 9 8 7 6 5 4 3
09 08 07 06

Typeset in 9.5pt Iowan by 70
Printed and bound in Great Britain by Henry Ling Limited, at the Dorset Press, Dorchester, DT1 1HD.

The publishers' policy is to use paper manufactured from sustainable forests.

Contents

Memo

Date: 11 October 2005

From: Derek Rowntree

To: All managers

Subject: Who needs a book of checklists?

Manager? Supervisor? Team leader? Superintendent? Co-ordinator? Section head? Executive officer? Chief this or senior that? Whatever they call you – if you are responsible for other people's work, then you are a manager and this book is for you.

Its systematic checklists will guide you and prompt your memory on most of the problem areas you'll face as a manager. In moments of stress and times of action it will give you the confidence that you are tackling things thoroughly. Even with fairly routine problems you will often find it offers you a stimulating 'second opinion'. And it will help you develop your managerial competences.

Why is the book needed?

Most of us get to be managers abruptly – without previous experience and often without training. The most successful are usually those who realize early on that there is something to be learned – and that it may not come naturally. They will spend some time thinking about the many *different* kinds of activity they are involved in each day in managing the work of other people. They will notice the areas in which they are less than satisfied with their own performances, and reflect on how they might improve. Where they can, they will discuss these managerial activities with other managers and maybe even with their own manager. And they will read books on aspects of management and take every opportunity to go on any courses and workshops that seem appropriate.

This book is meant to help all managers who are committed to such self-development. I have summed up what I have learned about managing and expressed it in the form of *checklists*. I myself find checklists easier to work with than the solid prose of most books on management – which may be fine if I'm seeking general inspiration, but hopeless if I'm looking for hints and tips about a problem that's currently troubling me.

How the book should help you

The checklists in this book should be equally helpful whether you are lucky enough to have had management training or have trained only in the 'school of hard knocks'. They are meant to:

- remind you of the *variety* of tasks and skills that make up this job of managing. (Nearly 50 areas are discussed and none of us is sufficiently adept in all of them.)
- help you to understand the problems that may confront you in each of these areas and develop appropriate competences.
- highlight the key factors that you may need to bear in mind in each area.
- indicate the main ways of proceeding within each area and, where appropriate, the advantages and disadvantages of each.
- give you practical frameworks for tackling common managerial problems.

- help you to be more systematic and thorough in your approach to each aspect of being a manager.
- give you a useful set of ideas around which you can discuss your experience with other managers.
- stimulate you to think about producing *your own* checklists – because I don't expect you to agree 100 per cent with mine, let alone find all you'll ever need in them.
- help you towards collecting the evidence you'll need to get your competences as a manager accredited, if that is what you want.

You will find the book contains two main kinds of checklists:

- **Analysis checklists** – to help you understand the problem area you find yourself in.
- **Action checklists** – to help you decide what needs doing and how best to do it.

So the checklists take you from analysis into action.

You may think it's a bit artificial trying to split the job of managing into quite separate areas of activity like this. As managers, running an operation, we're usually juggling finance, people, information, etc. – and all at the same time. But I think you'll find that taking the job apart like this will give you new insights – and that you'll be able to put the bits together again in a way that suits your own needs.

There is no need to read the sections in the order in which they are presented. Nor need you read the topics in any particular order. (You'll notice I occasionally refer you from one section or topic to another by printing the relevant title in **bold type**.) You could read through the book from first page to last, of course. This would be like a crash course in management. But more often I expect you will be coming to the book (or coming back to it) looking for help with some specific problem or task that's concerning you at that moment. And, if this is your own copy of the book, don't hesitate to make it even more your own by ticking boxes or pencilling in your own thoughts wherever it helps you to reflect on your experience of being a manager.

Managing your job

Contents

Introduction

Managing is about achieving results through the work of other people. On farms and in factories, in retail stores and in offices, in colleges and in hospitals, in theatres and in hotels, people are working in teams to produce results. And the person *responsible* for the work of each team – even if he or she is actually called supervisor, chief clerk, section leader, project director, executive officer, or whatever – is a manager.

Most managers start by being thrown in at the deep end. Your manager suddenly makes you an offer you can't refuse – to be in charge of your own team of staff. What 'being in charge' might mean may not be made entirely clear to you. Nor may you be told exactly what and who you are responsible for, what you are meant to do from day to day or how much freedom of action you have.

Your chances of being an effective manager depend to a large extent on how clearly you understand the nature of your job. So, in this chapter, our checklists enable you to analyze your own job and to think through some of the key issues that every manager has to face in getting their job done.

Analyzing your job

Managers are usually far too busy to reflect on their jobs. They are kept hard at it just getting through the daily workload. But when they do get a chance to reflect, they often decide they've been wasting a lot of time doing things they are not really expected to do – and perhaps neglecting certain things that are expected of them or that would be more worthwhile. Could this be true of you?

What is your job?

Consider the following questions carefully.

	Yes	No
● Does your job have a title?	❏	❏
● Are you sure to whom you are responsible?	❏	❏

	Yes	No

- Could you draw some sort of organization chart showing how your job connects up to other jobs in your organization? ❑ ❑

- Can you state the overall *purpose* of your job in a single sentence? ❑ ❑

- Can you be sure your manager would agree with that statement? ❑ ❑

- Can you state your 'timespan of discretion' – that is, how long you are allowed to carry on managing before someone checks on your results? ❑ ❑

- Do you have a job description, listing your duties and responsibilities? ❑ ❑

- Do you have a workplan, updated periodically in discussion with your manager, and setting out any specific tasks and targets expected of you – perhaps of your staff (your team) – in the months ahead? ❑ ❑

- Whether or not you have a job description or workplan (and without looking at it if you have) could you:

  - write a list of the *main duties* expected of you? ❑ ❑

  - rank those main duties in order of importance? ❑ ❑

  - list the staff, expenditure and other resources that you are responsible for? ❑ ❑

  - say in what circumstances you would need your manager's agreement before you could act on your decisions? ❑ ❑

  - list any specific tasks that you are expected to carry out as a matter of priority during the present year? ❑ ❑

  - list any specific objectives (involving quantities, quality, costs, target dates, etc.) that you are expected to attain during the present year? ❑ ❑

  - say what 'performance indicators' your manager will be looking for in order to appraise your effectiveness? ❑ ❑

	Yes	No
– say when your performance will next be formally appraised?	❏	❏
● Are you actually working in accordance with all the expectations mentioned above?	❏	❏
● If not, can you justify the fact that you are not?	❏	❏
● And is your manager aware of it?	❏	❏

N.B. If you feel uncomfortable about the number of times you have answered 'no' to the above questions, then your job is not as clear as you might prefer it to be. Perhaps this is something you should discuss with your manager.

The demands, constraints and choices of your job

Here is another way of looking at your job that may help you improve your effectiveness. Analyze it in terms of:

- the *demands* (which dictate what you *must* do);
- the *constraints* (which limit what you *can* do);
- your *choices* (which indicate how much freedom you have).

The demands of your job

	Yes	No
● Are there any regular activities that you cannot neglect (or delegate) without incurring some sort of penalty?	❏	❏
● Are there any specific targets you are required to meet?	❏	❏
● What is the source of these demands?		
– Your manager	❏	❏
– Colleagues at the same level as yourself in the organization	❏	❏
– The organization or 'the system' itself	❏	❏
– Your employees	❏	❏
– People outside the organization	❏	❏

	Yes	No
– Yourself (arising from your personal standards or ambitions)	❏	❏
● Can you rank these sources from 1–6 according to the importance of the demands they make on you? (Write the number to the *left* of each box.)	❏	❏
● Can you rank them according to how much attention you pay to them? (Write the rank number to the *right* of each box.)	❏	❏
● Do these rankings broadly match up – that is, are you paying more attention to the more important demands, and less to the less important?	❏	❏

● If not, what do you need to do about it? _____

_____

The constraints

What are the factors that *limit* you in what you would like to be able to do in your job?

● The attitudes or expectations of:
   – your manager   ❏
   – other managers   ❏
   – your employees   ❏
   – people outside the organization   ❏

● Your organization's policies or procedures   ❏

● Legal requirements   ❏

● Union agreements   ❏

● Shortage of skilled staff   ❏

● Shortage of other resources   ❏

● Inadequate technology (e.g. equipment or ways of working)   ❏

● The physical location of your section   ❏

● Your own skills, knowledge or attitudes   ❏

● Others_____

_____

Your choices

Finally, all managers have some degree of choice as to what work is to be done and how. Do you feel you ought to have *more* freedom than you have at present to decide on the following?

	Yes	No
● What work is to be done?	❑	❑
● When it is to be done	❑	❑
● How it is to be done	❑	❑
● The standards to which it is to be done	❑	❑
● The results that are to be achieved	❑	❑
● By whom the work is to be done	❑	❑
● Others _____		

KEY IDEA

If the above analysis reveals that your job is not what you think it ought to be, why not discuss your conclusions with your manager?

Managing versus operating

Do you spend enough of your time on managerial-type activities? Many managers find that much of their time is still taken up with the kinds of tasks they carried out *before* their promotion. They are still doing a fair bit of designing, producing, selling or whatever it is their team does. That is, they are still *operating* as well as managing. Your job is surely to manage operations, not to carry them out yourself.

Are you managing?

You can be sure you are managing if the bulk of your time is spent on deciding matters like the following. Tick those that you regularly make decisions about.

(a) What is to be achieved or produced ❑

(b) What work needs doing in order to achieve the
desired results ❑

(c) How the work will be done ❑

(d) When it must be done by ❑

(e) Who in your team will do the work ❑

(f) What resources or training they will need to do it ❑

(g) How you can support them in doing it well ❑

(h) How well the work *should* be done ❑

(i) How well the work *is* being done ❑

(j) What action needs to be taken if things are not going
as planned ❑

In short, you are managing if you are:

– **planning** the results to be obtained from other people's work –
(a) above;

– **organizing** them to get the necessary work done (**b–g**); and

– **monitoring** the outcomes of that work (**h** and **i**); with a view to

– **correcting** slippages from the plan – or taking advantage of new
opportunities (**j**).

(A)   What percentage of your working time is spent on deciding such matters as the ten listed above?

● Less than 25 per cent ❑

● 25–50 per cent ❑

● 50–75 per cent ❑

● More than 75 per cent ❑

Or are you still operating?

Here are some reasons why you might still be doing some operating. Tick
any that seem acceptable to you in *your* situation.

- I like to remind my team that I can do everything that I ask them to do ❑
- I can often do it better than they can ❑
- I don't want to lose the old skills ❑
- It helps me see things from the team's point of view ❑
- I want to show I haven't got swollen-headed ❑
- We'd never get through the daily load if I didn't do my bit ❑
- We'd never cope with the crises if I wasn't prepared to step in ❑
- I feel more comfortable operating than I do managing ❑
- It's part of my job description that I do some ❑
- Operating makes a relaxing change from managing ❑
- My manager (and/or other managers) does some operating and expects me to ❑

(B) What percentage of your working time is spent on operating?

- Less than 25 per cent ❑
- 25–50 per cent ❑
- 50–75 per cent ❑
- More than 75 per cent ❑

Yes   No

- Do your answers to **(A)** and **(B)** match up? (e.g. let's hope you're not claiming to spend more than 50 per cent of your time both on operating and on managing!) ❑ ❑

  Some management jobs do require the manager to do some operating. Others don't – yet the managers keep on operating regardless. This can reduce their effectiveness if it is done at the expense of their managing.

- Do you feel the percentage of time you devote to operating is about right? ❑ ❑

If not, what will you do about it? _____

_____

> **KEY IDEA**
>
> Don't let your operating interfere with your managing.

Managing your time

Time is the manager's greatest enemy. It is the one vital resource you can never get enough of. Like everyone else in the world (and in your organization) you get just 24 hours in a day and 365 days in a year. Yet some managers always seem pressed for time (working through lunch and taking home piles of paper) while others seem to have all the time in the world (and still get the job done).

The ability to *manage* their time is often what separates the good managers from the poor ones. (After all, if we can't organize ourselves, how can we be trusted to organize other people?) Yet few of us manage time as well as we should. In fact, we often don't manage it as well as we know how to manage it. We allow ourselves to get distracted by jobs that are more interesting than the priority tasks we realize we should be attending to first. We take on more work than we know we have time for. We are just too available to people who want us to work over problems they should really be thinking through for themselves. And so on.

The checklists in this section should help you value your time more, recognize what you are spending it on at present (and where it is being wasted), and consider a variety of ways of making more effective use of it. Underlying these checklists there are three basic ways of using time more effectively:

1 cutting out certain tasks;
2 working more efficiently;
3 planning how you will be using your time.

Most of the ideas in the checklists that follow will seem like common sense. Many of them you may be applying already. But all of us could benefit from applying just a few more of them – or applying them more rigorously!

How much is your time worth?

Many managers squander their time as if it were free. Have you ever worked out what your time costs per hour, or per minute? If not, try the following exercise. The sample figures in brackets show how the calculation would go for a manager earning £40,000 per year (which is all salary, with no bonuses or commission).

(a) Write down your annual salary (£40,000)

(b) Add on any regular bonus or commission (£40,000)

(c) Add on 25 per cent of your salary (a) for pension, national insurance, etc. (£50,000)

(d) Add on 100 per cent of your salary for overheads (office space, heat, light, telephone, technology, travel, secretarial and administrative help, etc.) (£90,000)

(e) Divide the total (d) by the number of working days in the year – probably about 230, after deducting weekends and holidays – to get your daily cost (£391)

(f) Divide your daily cost (e) by 8 to get your cost per hour (£49)

(g) Finally, divide your hourly cost (f) by 60 to get your cost per minute (82p)

Keep these last two figures firmly in mind when dealing with unwanted visitors or when you find yourself in meetings that seem to be getting nowhere. In fact, whatever you are doing, get into the habit of asking whether it is worth your cost per minute (g).

Cutting out busy work

One way of making better use of your time is to stop doing jobs you shouldn't be doing. Get rid of 'busy work' – work that keeps you busy but isn't really worth doing or could just as well be done by one of your staff. (See the checklists on **Managing versus operating**, page 6 and **Delegating**, pages 16–17.) Here are the key questions to ask.

	Yes	No
● Do I have a detailed job description?	❑	❑
● Do I know what my main goals and priorities are?	❑	❑
● Do I know the best sequence in which to do what must be done?	❑	❑
● Have I checked, in detail, how I spend each working hour in an average week?	❑	❑
● If not, am I prepared to keep a time log, recording what I do with each hour next week?	❑	❑
● Am I spending time operating rather than managing?	❑	❑
● Am I doing work that should be delegated to others?	❑	❑
● Am I doing things that needn't be done at all?	❑	❑
● Do I spend a big enough proportion of my time doing things that must be done and that only I can do?	❑	❑
● Do I concentrate on my main goals and priorities?	❑	❑
● Do I tackle them in the most appropriate sequence?	❑	❑

If your answers aren't what you know they should be, then only you will know what to do about it.

Stop wasting time

If you keep a log of your work (as suggested above), you'll soon see where time gets wasted. Here are some common ways of wasting time. Tick the *three* that cause you most trouble.

● Dealing with unwanted visitors	❑
● Other people's problems	❑
● Telephone interruptions	❑
● Social chit-chat	❑
● Unproductive meetings	❑
● Travelling	❑

- Too much irrelevant reading, internet browsing or paperwork ❑
- Endless drafting/redrafting of e-mails/memos/letters, etc. ❑
- Putting off difficult or boring tasks ❑
- Mislaying essential documents ❑
- Rectifying mistakes in your earlier work ❑
- Others _____

_____

The first few timewasters above we can blame partly on other people. The later ones are more our own responsibility. What can we do to prevent such waste? Below are some hints and tips. Are there a few suggestions here that you might usefully start using or use more often?

Callers

- Get a secretary or assistant to deal with unwanted visitors ❑
- Say 'no' more often (politely, of course) ❑
- Find an empty room in which to 'hide' for really top priority work ❑
- Make it clear when you will be available and unavailable to different kinds of people ❑
- See certain people only by appointment ❑
- Encourage staff not to come to you with problems until they have considered possible solutions ❑
- Don't do other people's thinking for them ❑
- Keep to the point in a conversation or discussion ❑
- Finish it as soon as usefully (and politely) possible ❑
- Ask your secretary to deal with or divert telephone calls ❑
- Have a set time of day for making/receiving phone calls ❑
- Be brisk and decisive when telephoning (try standing up rather than sitting) ❑

- Develop your own ways of signalling that your time is limited or that you must finish a conversation, e.g. 'I'm expecting a rather tricky call any minute, so I won't ask you to sit down', or 'I'm afraid I am due in a meeting' ❏
- A modicum of social chit-chat 'oils the wheels', but keep in mind the price of the lubricant ❏

Meetings

- Don't call for a meeting unless it has a purpose ❏
- Cancel any regular meeting if there is no business that can't wait till next time ❏
- Never enter a meeting without knowing what you want from it ❏
- If you're in charge of the meeting, make sure the group does not waste its time ❏
- If you're not, don't waste other people's time ❏
- Get taken off committees if your presence is not essential ❏

(See also the checklists on **Managing meetings**, page 218.)

Travelling

- Write, telephone or use videoconferencing technology instead ❏
- Get someone else to go ❏
- Get the other people to come to you ❏
- If you must go, plan the most cost-effective form of travel ❏
- If you can, use the travelling time either for catching up on some neglected chores or for deliberate relaxing (you may find it less irksome) ❏

Working practices

- Train someone else to decide which of the incoming paperwork or e-mails are worth your attention ❏

- Get taken off the circulation list for materials you don't need ❏
- Ask a member of your staff to summarize important documents ❏
- Encourage your staff to write memos etc. succinctly ❏
- Don't read everything with the same intensity – learn to skim and skip; pore over a text only if you're sure it's worth it ❏
- Don't write letters or memos if an e-mail or a telephone call will do ❏
- Don't have memos typed when a handwritten note will do ❏
- Jot down brief replies on memos you receive, photocopy if necessary, and return to the sender ❏
- If drafting is a headache, try speaking into a pocket recording device or using a word processor ❏
- Don't put off till tomorrow what needs doing today – think of the relief you'll feel when it's over and done with ❏
- Give yourself deadlines for completing tasks that you are dreading ❏
- Make sure other people know about those deadlines and will chivvy you to meet them ❏
- Have a filing system – with 'a place for everything and everything in its place' ❏
- Don't let the paperwork or e-mails pile up on your desktop: shift it (if only into the waste bin) ❏
- Be realistic about how long jobs are going to take you ❏
- Don't rush them and make mistakes that will plague you later ❏
- Don't take on more than you can handle properly ❏
- Plan your work for the days and weeks ahead ❏

N.B. If you've seen several suggestions that seem attractive, it may be wise not to try introducing them all at the same time. Consider introducing one or two new time-savers each week.

Planning your time

Like any other expensive resource, your time needs to be budgeted. What are you planning to work on tomorrow? Next week? Over the next month? You may not be in a position to think too far ahead. But at the very least you should begin *each working day* with clear intentions as to how you will spend it. Which of the following ideas are you already using or willing to try out?

	Yes	No
• Do you keep with you a diary noting appointments and meetings for the days ahead?	❑	❑
• Do you spend some time between one working day and the next thinking about:	❑	❑
– what you expect to be working on next day?	❑	❑
– and what you expect to achieve/complete?	❑	❑
• Do you make a written note of your daily workplan?	❑	❑
• Do you keep the plan where you can see it clearly throughout the working day?	❑	❑
• Does your plan distinguish between things you MUST do, and things you *could* do if you complete your priorities faster than you expect?	❑	❑
• Does your written workplan take the form of a timetable, splitting the day into 15 or 30 minute slots and showing what you plan to be doing in each?	❑	❑
• Do you take care to leave enough slack time in your daily plan for dealing with unforeseen problems?	❑	❑
• Do you allow for the possibility that you may be able to cope better with certain jobs during some parts of the day rather than others?	❑	❑

	Yes	No
• Are you realistic about how long you can devote yourself to one task (especially a creative one) before needing a change?	❏	❏
• Are you strict enough about building in a regular slot each day for your own 'thinking time' (as opposed to dealing with other people)?	❏	❏
• Do you review your plan at the end of each day, noting what has been accomplished and what must be continued next day (or later)?	❏	❏
• Can you learn from such reviews – about how realistic your time estimates are and what kinds of interruptions have prevented you from accomplishing all you planned?	❏	❏
• Can you find little treats to offer yourself for those days when you really did get it all done?	❏	❏
• Might it be worthwhile drawing up a schedule (less detailed, of course) about what you plan to be doing and completing for the next week/month/quarter?	❏	❏
• Might it be worthwhile encouraging some of your staff to make and display their own daily schedules?	❏	❏

KEY IDEA

Always keep in mind that day by day you have less and less time left in which to accomplish your heart's desire. Don't waste what time you have left and don't let others waste it for you.

Delegating

To manage is to achieve results by organizing *other people's work*. You cannot do all of your section's work by yourself. You have to share out the tasks. You will even need to set people tasks that you could do better than anyone else in your team. If you don't, you won't have time for the tasks that only you can do. (See the checklists on **Managing versus operating**, page 6.) Hence the need to delegate tasks.

But delegation is not just a matter of handing out tasks. If you tell people precisely how to carry out those tasks and give them no freedom to use their initiative, you are not delegating. Think of delegation as *entrusting* someone with the authority to *make decisions* about their task – and to act on their decisions.

You may, for example, specify what results you expect each of your team members to achieve – but leave it to them to decide what methods to use in achieving them. Or you may give examples of acceptable results without implying that only those would be acceptable. But the person to whom you've delegated is still responsible to you for what he or she is doing. And you will still be responsible to *your* manager for the work you have delegated. So you need to delegate with care and to watch out for progress and problems.

Many managers are *reluctant* to delegate. Others are *poor* delegators. Yet wise delegation can:

– increase the output of your team;

– make your team's work more satisfying;

– improve each member's competence;

– save you time for more productive tasks;

– demonstrate your ability as a manager;

– free you to move on to a more challenging job because you'll have developed competent team members who can take over from you.

The following checklists consider the barriers to successful delegation and how to overcome them.

Are you delegating enough?

	Yes	No
● Do you feel overburdened with duties?	❏	❏
● Do you find yourself having to work longer hours than most colleagues?	❏	❏

	Yes	No
● Do you regularly take work home?	❏	❏
● Does your team's work lose momentum if you are absent?	❏	❏
● Do you feel your staff come to you too frequently to ask about what they should be doing?	❏	❏
● Do you feel it necessary to check your team members' work in detail?	❏	❏
● Do you fear you are neglecting major long-term issues because you're too busy coping with day-to-day routines and crises?	❏	❏
● Do your staff think you don't let them use their initiative enough?	❏	❏

What stops you delegating?

	Yes	No
● Are you unsure of what you yourself are responsible for?	❏	❏
● Do you feel more at home with doing routine tasks than with planning, checking and controlling the work of other people?	❏	❏
● Do you insist on performing tasks you know you can perform better than other people in your team – even though this prevents you from performing tasks that none of them can perform as well as you?	❏	❏
● Do you fear that you will not appear 'busy' enough unless you are seen to be keeping your hand in at the same tasks as your team?	❏	❏
● Are you unsure of your team members' ability to take more responsibility for decisions about their work?	❏	❏
● Do you dread the thought of having to put right other people's mistakes?	❏	❏

	Yes	No
● Are you anxious about having to account to your manager or management colleagues for decisions made by your team members?	❑	❑
● Are you worried that your employees may undermine your authority or even challenge you for your job?	❑	❑

First steps in delegating

Whenever a new task or project comes up ask yourself:

	Yes	No
● Is this something I really *must* deal with myself? For example:		
– Patching up my own mistakes	❑	❑
– Disciplinary action	❑	❑
– Confidential matters	❑	❑

● If not, what knowledge or competence does the task
call for? _____

_____

	Yes	No
● Does anyone in my team have any or all of that knowledge/competence?	❑	❑
● If not, can I get one of them trained in time?	❑	❑
● Or can they learn on the job?	❑	❑
● Or can I recruit a capable person (if only temporarily)?	❑	❑
● Have I prepared my staff to accept more responsibility?	❑	❑

Whom to delegate to

● Which of my capable people is least overloaded?
● Who might benefit most from the new responsibility? (For example,
are there individuals with whom I could use it as a test of competence
or as a staff-development exercise?)

- How did likely individuals get on last time I delegated to them?
- How can I avoid unplanned delegation, e.g. through snap decisions in a meeting or a conversation?
- How can I guard against one of my staff taking on tasks that might be better done by someone else?
- How can I prevent my staff delegating tasks to *me*?

What am I delegating?

- What do I need to tell the individuals to whom I am delegating? For example:

	Yes	No
– how long the task will last	❏	❏
– any procedures I expect them to follow	❏	❏
– what kind of results I expect from them (e.g. objectives)	❏	❏
– how I propose to measure their performance	❏	❏
– how the task arose	❏	❏
– how the task fits into the work of the section and the organization	❏	❏
– what kinds of decisions each individual has authority to make and what resources he or she may use (e.g. money, materials and other staff)	❏	❏
– how and in what circumstances they are to report back to me	❏	❏

- How should I convey this information? For example:

	Yes	No
– conversation	❏	❏
– memo or e-mail	❏	❏
– written job description or workplan	❏	❏
– formal contract	❏	❏
• How can I check that individuals understand the nature and extent of what I have delegated?		
– Shall I quiz them about it?	❏	❏

    – What questions do they ask me? _____

	Yes	No
– Do they foresee any snags or difficulties?	❑	❑
● Do I need to make clear to the other team members:		
– just what I have delegated to the individual?	❑	❑
– in what areas is he/she now entitled to exercise authority?	❑	❑

Planning the delegation

	Yes	No
● Shall I delegate in stages – requiring successful completion of each stage before delegating the next?	❑	❑
● Can I and the individual to whom I'm delegating see the need for any special training/support?	❑	❑

● How can I best provide such training or support? _____

_____

● How much personal help shall I offer? (For example shall I decline to listen to a problem unless the individual has first written out one or two possible solutions?) _____

_____

● What sort of formal reporting system shall I set up to warn me of any likely departures from agreed standards or deadlines? _____

_____

● How else may I decide that I need to take some action?
For example:

	Yes	No
– unexplained delays	❑	❑
– missed targets	❑	❑
– my team member's worried manner	❑	❑
– his or her uncertainty or evasiveness	❑	❑
– other people's negative comments	❑	❑

    – others _____

_____

Managing the delegated task

	Yes	No
● Can I find ways of averting potential disasters without seeming so critical of the individual that he or she loses heart for delegation?	❏	❏
● Would it be valuable for me and the individual to sit down and systematically evaluate his or her performance in order to ensure that we both learn from the experience?	❏	❏
● If so:		
– at the end of the project?	❏	❏
– at intervals during a continuing task?	❏	❏
● Am I ready to learn about the difficulties my team members have faced, how I might have helped them more, and how they think I can help them develop from here?	❏	❏
● Am I prepared to relax my control (say, by allowing longer between reports) as the individual gains confidence and competence?	❏	❏
● Can I accept that the individual may perform the task quite adequately *without* doing it as I would have done it?	❏	❏
● Do I ensure that those team members who have responded well to delegation are those who will get any extra rewards that are going?	❏	❏

Does *your* manager delegate properly?

	Yes	No
● Does your manager delegate enough to you?	❏	❏
● Are there any parts of his/her job you would be happy to take responsibility for?	❏	❏
	Yes	No

	Yes	No
● When your manager does propose to delegate to you, you might usefully ask: Am I clear about just what is being delegated?	❏	❏
● Is it appropriate that he/she should delegate this task?	❏	❏
– Am I really the best available person to delegate this task to?	❏	❏
– Can I be sure of getting appropriate training and/or support?	❏	❏
– Am I clear (and happy) about the limits of my authority to take decisions without referring back to my manager?	❏	❏
– Do I know when/how I have to report to my manager?	❏	❏
– Can I see how the delegated task may contribute to my professional development?	❏	❏

How much and how well people delegate is a real test of their managerial ability. (See also the checklists on **Motivating your team**, page 146, and **Improving people's jobs**, page 142.) If they don't delegate enough, they're likely to run into the problems we discuss in the checklists on **Managing stress**, page 45. So, too, if they delegate poorly. The essence of management, once you've planned the work, is to get the right people doing it – and to keep yourself assured that they're continuing to do it right.

KEY IDEA

Always delegate as you would wish to be delegated to.

Understanding your organization

Organizations differ. Managing in a multinational bank is quite different from managing in one of a chain of retail stores, which is quite different again from managing in a hospital or a television company or a local government department.

Different organizations have their different ways of doing things and their different expectations of the people who work in them. This goes all the way from whether or not you call the manager by his or her first name and whether people wear formal clothes or casual ones at work, right through to the deeply held beliefs and expectations that people have about the organization and about one another's behaviour. In this section the checklists help you consider how your organization might differ from others in such respects and what you might need to do about it.

So what is *distinctive* about the organization you work in? Many different words have been used to refer to this distinctive 'feel' that each organization has – its 'climate', its 'personality', its 'ethos', its 'culture'.

Whatever the word, it means that you couldn't expect to go from being a manager in, say, an oil refinery or the armed services to being a manager in, say, an advertising agency or a computer software company and expect to relate in the same way to people elsewhere in the organization. The distinctive 'culture' of your organization will make its own demands and set its unique constraints on what you can do. You ignore it at your peril. So let's look into it with some checklists.

Where is the emphasis?

One way of understanding an organization is to ask what its goals appear to be. I am not talking here about its published goals or 'mission/vision statements'. Ask instead about its *informal* goals. What do people emphasize in their discussions and in their daily activities?

Look at each of the following possible emphases. Ask yourself, first of all, which of them are emphasized by your organization in general (**Org**). Then ask yourself which of them are emphasized within your section (**Sec**) Finally ask yourself which of them you would personally *prefer* to see emphasized (**Me**). Tick as many items as you wish.

	Org	Sec	Me
● Increasing output	❏	❏	❏
● Increasing size of market	❏	❏	❏
● Cutting out competitors	❏	❏	❏
● Increasing profits	❏	❏	❏

	Org	Sec	Me
● Decreasing costs	❑	❑	❑
● Gaining public prestige	❑	❑	❑
● Maintaining traditions	❑	❑	❑
● Innovation in products/methods	❑	❑	❑
● Employee satisfaction	❑	❑	❑
● Responsiveness to clients/customers	❑	❑	❑
● New technology	❑	❑	❑
● Highly professional management	❑	❑	❑
● Doing things by the book	❑	❑	❑
● Avoiding outside interference	❑	❑	❑
● Making a worthwhile difference in the world outside	❑	❑	❑
● Any others _____			

The self-image of your organization

Here is another aspect of your organization's culture. This time, we're not so much concerned with what your organization seems to emphasize but with how people *feel* about it and about working in it.

Which of the following words and phrases best reflect your colleagues' feelings? Again, consider first the organization generally, then your own section, and finally decide how you would *prefer* to be able to feel about the organization you work in. Tick as many as you like.

	Org	Sec	Me
● A good outfit to work in	❑	❑	❑
● OK, but not what it used to be	❑	❑	❑
● Getting better all the time	❑	❑	❑
● Definitely going downhill	❑	❑	❑
● Warm, friendly and relaxed	❑	❑	❑
● Cold, conflict-ridden and stressful	❑	❑	❑

	Org	Sec	Me
● Making a worthwhile contribution to society	❏	❏	❏
● Efficient and effective	❏	❏	❏
● Carrying on a proud tradition	❏	❏	❏
● Expanding and optimistic	❏	❏	❏
● Defensive and pessimistic	❏	❏	❏
● Innovative and opportunistic	❏	❏	❏
● Established and complacent	❏	❏	❏
● Entrepreneurial and go-getting	❏	❏	❏
● Uncertain and apologetic	❏	❏	❏
● Encouraging of individual initiative	❏	❏	❏
● Stifled by red tape and heavy management	❏	❏	❏
● Any other descriptions _____			

Time and tempo

Organizations differ greatly in how far they look ahead, and in the speed at which they work. So do sections within them. How would you describe your organization and your section? And what would be your personal preferences? Tick as many as you wish.

How far ahead do plans extend?

	Org	Sec	Me
● Days	❏	❏	❏
● Weeks	❏	❏	❏
● Months	❏	❏	❏
● Years	❏	❏	❏

How would you describe the *tempo* of work?

● Lethargic and apathetic	❏	❏	❏
● Slow but steady	❏	❏	❏
● Busy but rarely overstretched	❏	❏	❏

	Org	Sec	Me
● Sometimes slow/sometimes frantic	❏	❏	❏
● Staggering from crisis to crisis	❏	❏	❏
● So frantic or erratic as to be counter-productive	❏	❏	❏
● Other descriptions _____			

Who exercises influence?

Which of the following people make decisions or express views that have noticeable effects on the overall quality of working life within your organization and/or within your section? Use the **Me** column to indicate any groups that you would like to see being more (+) or less (–) influential.

	Org	Sec	Me
● Individual employees	❏	❏	❏
● Supervisors	❏	❏	❏
● Junior and middle line managers	❏	❏	❏
● Senior line managers	❏	❏	❏
● Staff specialists (e.g. in personnel or accounts)	❏	❏	❏
● Outside consultants	❏	❏	❏
● Directors	❏	❏	❏
● Shareholders	❏	❏	❏
● Customers/clients	❏	❏	❏
● Suppliers	❏	❏	❏
● Trade unions	❏	❏	❏
● Government	❏	❏	❏
● Pressure groups or individual opinion leaders	❏	❏	❏
● Other outside organizations _____			

● Others _____

Leadership styles

Which of the following terms and phrases best describe the most typical styles of leadership in your organization and in your section? And which would you *prefer* to see *more* of (+)?

	Org	Sec	Me
● Formal and bureaucratic	❑	❑	❑
● Informal and flexible	❑	❑	❑
● Consultative and encouraging participation	❑	❑	❑
● Authoritarian and directive	❑	❑	❑
● Concerned primarily with getting the job done	❑	❑	❑
● Concerned primarily with helping people develop	❑	❑	❑
● About equally concerned with the job and people	❑	❑	❑
● Overdemanding and exploitative	❑	❑	❑
● Demanding but reasonable	❑	❑	❑
● Ill-informed and autocratic	❑	❑	❑
● Supportive and stimulating	❑	❑	❑
● Paternalistic and patronizing	❑	❑	❑
● Other descriptions _____			

Human relationships

Organizations differ greatly in the kinds of relationships they produce among their staff – making the place more or less congenial to work in. How is it within your organization/section? And what would you like to see less of (–) and more of (+)?

Do people, in general:

	Org	Sec	Me
Like each other?	❏	❏	❏
Share common beliefs?	❏	❏	❏
Have common goals?	❏	❏	❏
Trust one another?	❏	❏	❏
Work co-operatively?	❏	❏	❏
Help one another out?	❏	❏	❏
Exchange confidences?	❏	❏	❏
Protect one another's interests?	❏	❏	❏
Take pride in one another's skills and achievements?	❏	❏	❏
Meet outside work?	❏	❏	❏
Other positive features _____			

Or do they, in general:

	Org	Sec	Me
Dislike one another?	❏	❏	❏
Disagree on many important matters?	❏	❏	❏
Have conflicting goals?	❏	❏	❏
Suspect or fear one another?	❏	❏	❏
Try to gain at one another's expense?	❏	❏	❏
Withhold help from one another? Hinder one another where possible?	❏	❏	❏
Denigrate or ignore one another's skills and achievements?	❏	❏	❏
Avoid each other outside work?	❏	❏	❏
Other negative features _____			

The communication pattern

How would you describe the general style of communication within your organization? Tick as many of the boxes in the first two columns as seem to apply. And again, what would you particularly like to see less of (–) and more of (+)?

	Org	Sec	Me
• Candid and open	❏	❏	❏
• Suspicious and cliquish	❏	❏	❏
• Bureaucratically controlled	❏	❏	❏
• Haphazard	❏	❏	❏
• Defensive or power-seeking	❏	❏	❏
• Purposely evasive or misleading	❏	❏	❏
• Grapevine very important	❏	❏	❏
• Poor communication down from managers	❏	❏	❏
• Good communication down from managers	❏	❏	❏
• Poor communication upwards	❏	❏	❏
• Good communication upwards	❏	❏	❏
• Poor communication between sections	❏	❏	❏
• Good communication between sections	❏	❏	❏
• Communication is generally:			
– reliable	❏	❏	❏
– unreliable	❏	❏	❏
– helpful/supportive	❏	❏	❏
– critical/discouraging	❏	❏	❏
• Other styles			

Who does well?

This final checklist touches on a very important aspect of the climate or culture of your organization. What kinds of people get on well – both in terms of job satisfaction and of promotion – in your organization and in your section? And which of them would you particularly like to see less (–) or more (+) rewarded?

The people who get on well are those who:

	Org	Sec	Me
● Are technically competent and work hard	❏	❏	❏
● Produce more than others	❏	❏	❏
● Suck up to the managers	❏	❏	❏
● Show loyalty to the organization	❏	❏	❏
● Avoid making trouble for management	❏	❏	❏
● Stick meticulously to the rules	❏	❏	❏
● Look after their own interests	❏	❏	❏
● Seek power and manipulate others	❏	❏	❏
● Help others to develop	❏	❏	❏
● Generate useful ideas	❏	❏	❏
● Earn the respect of colleagues	❏	❏	❏
● Earn the respect of people outside the organization	❏	❏	❏
● Other descriptions _____			

In this section we have considered a number of facets of organizational life. Maybe your organization has yet other facets worth thinking about in the same sort of way.

1 I asked you to tick off the best descriptions of how things are in your organization generally and in your section in particular.
   (a) Did you usually find you were ticking off the same items for both? If so, the 'ethos' or 'culture' in your section is presumably pretty similar to that in the organization as a whole. This would suggest that people in your section are probably well-integrated with the rest of the organization and don't have too much trouble relating to other sections.

(b) But what if your ticks didn't match up too well? This would suggest that your section, is to some extent, at odds with the culture of the organization. Do you think this is so? Does it cause problems? Does anything need doing about it? (If so, do you think things should change within your section, within the organization, or both?) Can anything be done about it? (And if not – or not in the short run – what can you do, as manager, to ensure that your section and the organization do not suffer unduly because of it?)

2 I also asked you to indicate *your own* preferences.

(a) If, in general, you ticked all three boxes for the same items then you are very fortunate. Both your section and your organization would seem to have the kind of culture you prefer.

(b) But what if your ticks indicate that your preferences tally with what is typical of the organization but *not* of your section? Maybe you need to do some work on transforming the culture in your section? Or maybe you'd be happier working elsewhere in the organization? What do you think?

(c) And if your preferences tended to agree with the culture of your section but differ from those of the organization, then you are in the same position outlined in **1(b)** above. What, if anything, can be done about it?

(d) Finally, if your preferences differ from what is common both in your section and in the organization as a whole, you do seem to have a problem. Are you really so at odds with all those around you? If so, you might be happier (though I can't guarantee it) working for a different kind of organization altogether.

What you make of this kind of analysis is up to you. But it is important that you take it seriously and go through it again from time to time. Organizations are constantly changing. Cultures evolve. New brooms come in and sweep differently. Old worms suddenly decide to turn. The manager who is unaware of the consequent changes in 'culture' can be left stranded and impotent.

KEY IDEA

To be an effective manager of your team, you must maintain a realistic understanding of the changing culture of your organization.

Mastering the politics

As a manager you will want to get things done in your organization. If you want to get things done you need to wield influence. In order to wield influence you need to have some power. If you haven't enough power of your own, you'll need the support of other people with power. You may also need to counteract the influence of certain powerful people whose wishes run counter to your own.

In short, you need to understand who has what kind of power in your organization and how it gets used. That's organizational politics.

The dirty face of organizational politics is the scheming and self-seeking and back-biting that advances certain individuals' careers or sectional interests regardless of (or against) the best interests of the organization.

The acceptable and inevitable face is the struggle between individuals and groups who all have the best interests of the organization at heart, but disagree as to what they are and how they might best be attained.

The following checklists should help you understand the political manoeuvrings within your own organization, and do what you can to develop the power you need.

Where does power come from?

There are at least eight sources of power. Do you have one or more of the following? If so, rank them from 1 to whatever, according to which you have most and least of.

- **Resource power:** yours because you have some resources (money, staff, facilities, etc.) which are desired by other people and which you can bestow on them if they do as you wish. ❏

- **Information power:** yours because you have access to inside information (e.g. about what is going on behind the scenes) that enables you to act more effectively than those who are not in the know. ❏

- **Position power:** yours purely because you have a recognized role and title within the organization (and probably needing to be backed up by one of the other forms of power). ❏

- **Proxy power:** yours because you represent some person or group whom the people you are dealing with dare not go against. ❏

- **Expert power:** yours because other people choose to act as you suggest in areas in which they accept that you know more than they do. ❏

- **Personality power:** yours because you have (at least for the time being) some kind of charisma or self-confidence or sense of mission that persuades people to go along with you. ❏

- **Physical power:** yours because there is something about, say, your powerful physique, dominating body language or deep and resonant voice that unnerves or intimidates people and makes them defer to your wishes. ❏

- **Favour power:** yours because you have done favours for people in the past so you can call on them to repay by lending you their power when you need it. ❏

- Which one of the above sources of power would you most like to acquire more of?

  _____

- Which of them do you believe you might be able to acquire more of? _____

  _____

Who exercises what power?

Which of the types of power listed above do you have to cope with from the people you regularly have dealings with?

- Your manager _____

_____

- Your manager's manager _____

_____

- Your fellow managers _____

_____

- Your team members _____

_____

- Other people in the organization _____

_____

- People outside the organization _____

_____

Power can be used for good or for ill. In which of the following ways do you see power being used by your manager (**B**), by your fellow managers (**F**) and by your employees (**S**)?

	B	**F**	**S**
• To gain more than their fair share of whatever benefits are available	❏	❏	❏
• To block other people's legitimate and worthwhile workplans	❏	❏	❏
• To set people against one another	❏	❏	❏
• To seek more and more power for the sake of it	❏	❏	❏
• To pursue personal advancement at the expense of the organization	❏	❏	❏
• To make themselves immune to criticism	❏	❏	❏
• To prevent other people advancing themselves	❏	❏	❏
• To pursue personal vendettas	❏	❏	❏
• To always remind people how powerful they are, even if they have nothing to gain on a particular occasion	❏	❏	❏

- Other ways _____

_____

There are many different tactics people use when exercising power for dubious purposes. Which of the following tactics do you see in your organization?

- Withholding information from people who
  need it ❑
- Distorting the information ❑
- Circulating slanderous gossip ❑
- Passing off other people's ideas as their own ❑
- Working to rule (e.g. go-slows) ❑
- Inventing new rules to restrict other people ❑
- Reinterpreting the existing rules to ease their own
  freedom of action ❑
- Empire-building ❑
- Espionage and infiltration of other groups ❑
- Fostering a climate of 'them' versus 'us' ❑
- Forming cliques and in-groups ❑
- Agreeing not to reveal the skeletons in one another's
  cupboards ❑
- Blackmail ❑
- Sabotage ❑
- Physical violence (or threats of) ❑
- Other tactics _____

_____

_____

So, do you have a clearer idea about who exercises what kind of power for what purposes and through what tactics? This may be your first step towards deciding whether it is in the best interests of yourself, your section and the organization to go along with them or to fight back.

How to acquire more power

The only way of fighting other people's power is to acquire more yourself (or at least make maximum use of what you've already got). In general terms, the ways of acquiring more power can be deduced from the list of sources of power on pages 33–34 – get control of resources, gather information, become an acknowledged expert, do people favours and so on.

Here are some specific hints and tips. Which of them would you feel comfortable about applying in your situation?

- Identify all the powerful people and opinion leaders whose goodwill you and your team might at some time or other be able to benefit from. (Remember that some of these may be behind the scenes, e.g. secretaries and assistants) ❏

- Find out what each of these people would welcome by way of 'favours' – respect, more resources, help with difficult managers or members of staff, etc. ❏

- Provide such favours where you feel it is not unethical or disloyal to other colleagues to do so ❏

- At all events, avoid antagonizing such people unless you feel some greater purpose is at stake ❏

- Join the unofficial networks of staff (the sports club, the community service group, the drama group, etc.) that cut across the formal hierarchy of the organization, giving you access to inside information and personal support that you would not get as the occupant of your official position in the hierarchy ❏

- Do deals with other individuals or groups who will give you support in what you are after, provided you do the same for them ❏

- Persuade people to support you by making out a good case for what you want done and, where possible, showing how they and/or the organization will gain ❏

- If a particular individual seems resistant to your arguments, arrange for that individual to be approached by one or more people he or she respects who happen to be your supporters ❏

- Volunteer for the kinds of tasks and projects that give you control of more resources and/or access to more powerful people and/or enable you to develop more expertise ❏

- With each new increase in your power, ask yourself how it can be used to gain you yet more power ❏

- Let it be seen that you use what power you have in an open, responsible and public-spirited fashion – and not for self-aggrandizement and personal gain ❏

- Where possible, undermine the power of those pursuing dubious ends by bringing their political chicanery out into the open ❏

- Other hints and tips _____

KEY IDEA

Don't feel you must seek sufficient power to vanquish all who oppose you; such people's goals will often be at least as justifiable as yours.

Negotiating

Not many law abiding managers are in a position these days to make people 'an offer they can't refuse'. So we have to negotiate. If we want something from them, we have to be prepared to give something they want in return.

By its nature, negotiation arises out of a conflict of interests. If you are buying a car, you want to pay the lowest possible price and the sellers want to get the highest possible price. However, the sellers will be prepared to accept less than their asking price and you will be prepared to pay more than your first offer. If the maximum you would pay is higher than the minimum they would accept, then it should be fairly easy to negotiate an agreed price within this range. The difficulties begin when your maximum is less than their minimum. Anything you gain will be at their loss, and vice versa.

None of us likes to lose, so one of the aims of negotiation – especially if both parties will be working together in the future – is to find a way for *both* to gain something they value. That is, successful negotiation is not always a matter of trying to get yourself the best possible deal – 'I win, you lose'. In the long term you may do better to settle for a 'win–win' compromise that enables both parties to save face and meet again on amicable terms.

You may be involved in trade union negotiations over pay and conditions. You may be involved in bargaining with customers or suppliers, perhaps for the price and terms on which goods or services are to be supplied. You may even find yourself bargaining with your manager or with other managers in your organization – say for the use of resources or the freedom to make certain decisions. Whatever kind of negotiation or bargaining you need to do, the following checklists should offer some guidance.

The ground rules of negotiation

When negotiations are carried out by specialists, there are usually a number of agreed conventions, which may not apply if you are bargaining with, say, other managers in your own organization.

The following conventions or ground rules are fairly common in trade union negotiations, but many of them would apply in other negotiations also. Which of them would be relevant to the kind of negotiating *you* might be doing?

- Whatever happens during negotiation, both parties hope to reach a mutually acceptable agreement ❏

- Each side is expected to be willing to move from its original proposal, offer or position ❏

- Negotiation is likely to proceed through a series of offers and counter-offers towards a settlement that gives something of value to both sides ❏

- Firm offers must be clearly distinguished from provisional offers ❑
- Firm offers, unlike provisional offers, must not be withdrawn once they have been made ❑
- Similarly, concessions must not be withdrawn once they have been made ❑
- Strong words, expressions of incredulity and apparent exasperation are accepted as legitimate bargaining tactics and do not cast doubt on either party's good faith ❑
- Private off-the-record discussions may be used to clarify points and probe one another's positions ❑
- Such discussions should not be referred to in the official negotiation unless both sides have so agreed ❑
- No third party should be brought into the discussion unless both sides have agreed that further progress will otherwise be impossible ❑
- The terms of the final agreement should be clearly understood by both parties (no 'pulling a fast one'), and will be implemented as written ❑
- The final agreement should enable both sides to claim that they have gained something of value and so, despite what they have conceded, save face ❑

Preparing for negotiation

Here are some questions to consider before you meet your 'opponents' across the bargaining table.

- What are we going to negotiate about?
- Do I know all the issues my opponents are likely to raise?
- Do they know all the issues I am likely to raise?
- What is the ideal settlement I would like to achieve?
- What is the worst I would agree to settle for?

- Realistically, what do I think I have a good chance of achieving?
- What concessions might I be able to offer to improve my chances of getting more of what I want?
- What answers do I think my opponents would give to the questions above?
- Do I need to meet my opponents informally to sound out their position (and impress them with the strength of my own)?
- What should be my opening offer or demand?
- Will it leave me enough room for manoeuvre?
- What arguments am I going to use in support of my case?
- What benefits might my opponents get from accepting my case?
- What unpleasant effects might they suffer by accepting it?
- How shall I deal with their objections to these effects?
- What is the weakest point of my case?
- How shall I counter my opponents if they pick on this weakness?
- Do I need to assemble more facts and figures?
- What do I know of my own strengths and weaknesses as a negotiator?
- What can I do to build on the strengths and minimize the weaknesses?
- Do I need to work with colleagues as a negotiating *team*? (Don't let yourself be outnumbered.)
- If so, what should be the different roles of the team members?
- What are my opponents' strengths and weaknesses?
- How can I counter their strengths and/or exploit their weaknesses?
- Is there anything I can do now to strengthen my position?
- Is there anything I can do to stop my opponents strengthening theirs?

The bargaining

Every negotiation is unique. So you cannot expect to write the script in advance. There are, however, a few typical approaches and ploys you may want to draw on and combine as seems appropriate:

1 Open by asking for more than you expect to get, or by making it clear that your opponents cannot expect to get all they would like.

2 Let your opponents do plenty of talking – while you listen actively and observe their body language.

3 Try to work out what meaning lies behind what your opponents say – e.g. does their 'no' mean 'maybe' and their 'maybe' mean 'yes'?

4 Ask plenty of questions to challenge their position and assess how far they may be bluffing.

5 Be non-committal about their proposals and explanations.

6 Aim to convince your opponents that your case is so strong that you scarcely need to consider offering them concessions.

7 If you offer a concession, make it conditional – e.g. 'I will consider doing so-and-so if you will do such-and-such'.

8 Don't reach final agreement on one of the issues at stake until all the issues have been considered and can be traded off against one another in the final settlement.

9 Never allow discussion of concessions you couldn't possibly make or hint at sanctions you couldn't or wouldn't impose.

10 Avoid hectoring your opponents or trying to make them look foolish.

11 Speak as firmly and assertively as may be necessary but don't lose your temper.

12 If you need time to think or gather more information, call for 'time out'.

13 Unless you are prepared to win at all costs (including making permanent enemies of your defeated opponents), look for ways to help them preserve their dignity.

14 Be ready to use or to counter ploys like the following:
   ● The *Time's getting on* ploy – suggesting (rightly or wrongly) that a settlement must be reached quickly.
   ● The *Yes, but* . . . ploy – acceptance of one part of the opponents' proposal, but on terms that may not be acceptable.
   ● The *Believe it or not* ploy – a straight bluff ('I've already had a better offer'), which should be called (e.g. 'So why don't you take it?').

- The *Or else* ploy – a straight threat ('I'll take my business elsewhere if we can't agree'). Best ignored, and never uttered unless you really mean it.
- The *Divide and rule* ploy – trying to get agreement on issues one by one so as to reduce your opponents' room for the kind of manoeuvre mentioned in (**8**) above.
- The *Think of your reputation* ploy – suggesting that your opponents will lose credibility unless they agree to your proposals.
- The *Trust me* ploy – 'Go along with me now and I'll do what I can to get what you want later'. (Promises, promises!)
- The *Beyond my remit* ploy – suggesting that if your opponents want to dispute certain issues, it will delay or complicate matters because you'll need to take advice from others outside the meeting.

15 Move towards closing the negotiation by:
   - making your absolutely final offer (so long as it really is);
   - offering a concession if your opponents will agree to settle at a position you can accept;
   - suggesting you split the difference between what they want and what you want;
   - coming up with new incentives for them to move closer to your position;
   - suggesting new sanctions that may apply if they fail to move closer;
   - spelling out the ways in which your opponents can claim to have gained from the settlement you propose.

Dos and don'ts of negotiation

Finally, here are some suggestions based on studies (by the Huthwaite Research Group of Sheffield, UK) of the behaviours avoided and the behaviours used by people known to be skilled negotiators. Which of them strike you as usable in your kinds of negotiations?

- Don't use irritating phrases like 'our fair and reasonable proposal' – which imply the other side is being unfair and unreasonable. ❏

- If you feel you must launch an attack on your opponents, do it abruptly – rather than building up to it in a way that allows them time to develop a counter-attack. ❏

- Use your strongest argument *on its own* (rather than saying 'Here are ten reasons why . . .'). ❏

- Don't immediately make a counter-proposal when your opponents make a proposal. ❏

- Tell your opponents when you are about to make a proposal or ask them a question ('I would like to propose . . .' or 'I would like to ask you . . .'). ❏

- Tell the other side *why* you are proposing, asking or doing something (to allay any suspicions or misconceptions they may have about your motives). ❏

- If you want to disagree with your opponents, mention your reasons first (or they may not get listened to). If they are accepted you may not have to point out that you disagree. ❏

- Ask a lot of questions (enabling you to gather information, gain thinking time and impress your opponents with your concern for their views and needs). ❏

- Summarize the discussion and spell out the implications of everything each side seems to have agreed to – so that you don't leave the negotiation with a glossed-over agreement that will break down in the real world. ❏

- Assess your own performance afterwards in terms of what you did and what you might have done better, and why. ❏

KEY IDEA

Don't try to negotiate your opponents into the ground. Leave them, as the saying goes, 'at least the price of the bus fare home'.

Managing stress

Most managers are under pressure. Too much to do – too little time and too few resources to do it with. Up to a point, we can tolerate such pressure, even thrive on it. It keeps us on our toes, gives us a challenge and adds to the zest of our work.

But too much is too much. When the pressure becomes too intense and/or goes on too long, our energy gives out. We lose heart. We get anxious and begin to doubt our ability to win through. We start making errors of judgement. The pressure has turned into *stress*.

Individuals differ in how they react. The point at which pressure becomes stress will vary from one to another. But we all have our breaking point. And once we start experiencing regular stress, we risk losing our effectiveness as managers. We also risk ulcers, high blood pressure, strokes and heart attacks. As they say, death is only Nature's way of telling us to slow down. Best we tell ourselves first.

So it is important for managers to recognize the early signs of stress and to learn ways of coping with it. Our primitive ancestors knew just two ways of responding to a threat – fight or flight. Neither of these is very helpful to the more subtle threats that can make life stressful for the modern manager. One's unduly demanding manager cannot be dealt with in quite the same way as a charging bull. So we need to discuss other ways of dealing with stress – minimizing it or, preferably, avoiding it. That is what the checklists in this section are about.

Pressure versus stress

Here are some questions that should help you decide whether you are merely under pressure or are beginning to experience stress. Are the following descriptions true of you more than 50 per cent of the time, less than 50 per cent or, indeed, never at all?

	More than 50 per cent	Less than 50 per cent	Never
● Do you feel overworked?	❏	❏	❏
● Are you irritated by other people's incompetence?	❏	❏	❏
● Do you feel like hitting people instead of telling them what is bothering you?	❏	❏	❏
● Do you become withdrawn, morose or difficult to talk to?	❏	❏	❏
● Do you put off making important decisions?	❏	❏	❏
● Do you have doubts about your decisions once you've made them?	❏	❏	❏
● Do you find it difficult to delegate work?	❏	❏	❏
● Do you feel you could never cope without tobacco, alcohol or other drugs?	❏	❏	❏
● Do you feel uneasy when you are not working?	❏	❏	❏
● Do you feel tense and restless, and find it hard to relax?	❏	❏	❏
● Do you feel anxious and panicky?	❏	❏	❏
● Do you get depressed for no obvious reason?	❏	❏	❏
● Do you find it hard to concentrate?	❏	❏	❏
● Do you respond badly to criticism?	❏	❏	❏
● Are you overtired and unable to sleep?	❏	❏	❏
● Do you feel your work is no longer worthwhile?	❏	❏	❏
● Do you feel you are not really up to your job?	❏	❏	❏

	More than 50 per cent	Less than 50 per cent	Never
● Do you feel there is no one with whom you can discuss your real feelings?	❑	❑	❑
● Do you worry about the state of your health?	❑	❑	❑
● Are you relieved when a health problem forces you to stay off work for a day or two?	❑	❑	❑
● Do you feel that food is tasteless, hard to get down, or just not worth bothering with?	❑	❑	❑
● Do you wish you had a less responsible job?	❑	❑	❑
● Do you fear you may lose your job?	❑	❑	❑
● Do you feel that life itself is getting too much for you?	❑	❑	❑

If you answered 'never' to all the above questions, then I think you're kidding yourself. (Another question: Do you pretend to yourself that things aren't as bad as they are?) All of us have some of those feelings some of the time. But if you answered 'more than 50 per cent' to more than six, then you may already be under too much stress. Perhaps you should have a talk with your doctor before it's too late.

Ways to minimize or avoid stress

Even a few doubtful answers to the questions above may indicate that you are not coping with stress as well as you might. Here are some hints and tips to help you do better. Tick those you are not using already but think you ought to try.

Within the job

● Admit to yourself when things are getting too much for you.   ❑

- Learn to say 'no' to irksome tasks that could just as well be done by someone else. ❏

- Try to deter other people from passing their crises on to you. ❏

- Delegate more. ❏

- Without being totally inflexible, establish some degree of routine in your working life. ❏

- Arrange at least half an hour a day when you can think things over with absolutely no interruptions. ❏

- Keep your list of priorities firmly in mind or, preferably, on display where you are working. ❏

- Don't waste time on low-priority tasks when you know you should be at least making a start on some of higher priority. ❏

- Try to pace your work, plan ahead and tackle potential problems before they blow up into crises, impossible deadlines and sheer panic. ❏

- Learn to lose a few battles without feeling you are losing face. (You win some; you lose some.) ❏

- Be tolerant about your own mistakes – will anyone care a hundred years from now, or even a hundred days? ❏

- Try to find as much fun as possible in your work, and aim to have plenty of laughs (even if they're often at your own expense). ❏

Looking after yourself

- Pay attention to the messages your body sends you – palpitations, migraines, upset stomach, etc. ❏

- Get plenty of sleep – some need more than eight hours a night and some less; make sure you get as much as you need. (But don't let yourself come to rely on sleeping pills.) ❏

- If you know you would benefit from a 15-minute nap in the middle of the day, do your best to take one. ❏

- Take exercise several times a week – whatever seems sensible for your age and condition (walking, jogging, swimming, golf). Working your muscles will invigorate your mind. ❏

- Try to find 20 minutes every day in which you sit or lie down and systematically tense up and then relax every muscle in turn from your toes to your scalp – your mind may loosen up also. ❏

- Regard it as part of your managerial responsibility to take regular holidays and forget about the job. ❏

- Spend time with friends and family and try to ensure that you have some absorbing interest outside your organization. ❏

- Don't get so competitive in your sports and pastimes (either with others or with yourself) that they become stressful too. ❏

- Avoid self-pity, the escalating use of alcohol (or other drugs) and the company of moaners. ❏

- Make a list of your fears and the possible happenings you most dread – and be realistic about how likely they are to befall you. (As Mark Twain said, 'I have suffered a great many calamities, but most of them never happened.') ❏

- Talk your fears over with someone you trust who can help you get them into perspective. ❏

- If your job really does get too stressful, seek a demotion – claiming, if you like, that you need more time for your family and other outside interests. ❏

KEY IDEA

Look out for signs of stress in your team members also. You may be the cause of it.

CHAPTER TWO

Managing operations

Contents

Introduction

Every manager is involved in running an operation. He or she may, for example, be concerned with getting books published, or tourists to their holiday destinations, or patients treated in hospital, or students provided with a quality education, or crime prevented, detected and punished. An operation is any activity or project designed to help achieve an organization's objectives and ensure that customers or clients are satisfied with the products or services you provide.

So, you will need to be clear about your customers' or clients' needs and how to assure them of a quality product or service. You will need to plan how to meet your customers' or clients' needs – working in terms of objectives – to keep checking that your plans are turning out as expected, to make decisions about how to correct or progress the operation and to ensure that your team is keeping up the appropriate standards of quality.

To do all of this, you will need to exercise leadership. And, from time to time, you will need to introduce change in what your team does or the way it does it – with a view to running your operation more productively or more efficiently.

Of course, managing an operation also involves **Managing people** (page 111), **Managing finance** (page 103) and **Managing information** (page 185). But they're all such big issues in their own right that I've given each a separate section in this book. I hope you'll agree with me that the topics I've mentioned in the paragraph above are quite enough to be going on with for the moment. Anyway, the checklists in this section provide a basis on which you can build in other sections.

Satisfying customer needs

'This would be a great place to work if it wasn't for the shoppers/audiences/ passengers/students/patients/guests, etc.!' I expect you've heard remarks like that as often as I have. They're said jokingly (usually), but they do sometimes betray a feeling that customers or clients should be there for the speaker's benefit rather than vice versa.

And yet we all have experience of *being* customers. We all know what an infuriating experience it can sometimes be. Haven't we all known what it is like to be ignored by sales staff, to be deceived about what is on offer, to be given something other than what we asked for (often much later than we were told we'd get it), to have our complaints met with resistance or feeble excuses – in general to be treated as of little account by the people who are supposedly providing us with some sort of goods or services?

But things are maybe changing. People everywhere are spending their resources more cautiously. More and more people now believe that they have 'consumer rights', and there is usually no shortage of suppliers for them to choose among. So most will choose to buy their goods and services from organizations that clearly try to satisfy their needs and treat them with proper respect.

Maybe your organization already has a clear customer/client service policy. Whether it has or not, what can *you* do to help ensure that people keep coming back for your goods or services? How can you be sure of satisfying their needs (and thereby keeping you and your colleagues in work)?

Who are your customers?

Many organizations – like hospitals, colleges and government departments – were once scarcely aware that they had customers. But most have now realized that all the people we are providing with goods or services are our customers – even if they are not paying us for them out of their own pockets. It is their needs we must satisfy. (And not all of these customers will come from outside our organization.)

External customers

Taking your own organization, can you think of examples of customers in some or all of the following categories?

	Yes	No
● People who may only need what you are offering very rarely, perhaps only once in a lifetime	❏	❏

	Yes	No
• Potential customers or clients who have yet to realize what you can offer them	❏	❏
• Regular purchasers who use your services frequently	❏	❏
• Customers of rival organizations who have a less favourable image of your organization	❏	❏
• People who were once your customers but are not any longer	❏	❏
• People who pay for your services on behalf of other people	❏	❏
• Large-scale customers with considerable power over your organization	❏	❏
• Other people whose decisions influence what your organization can do (e.g. government)	❏	❏
• Others _____		

Internal customers

Now, what about people *inside* your organization who mostly won't be paying you directly for whatever it is they depend on you for? For example:

	Yes	No
• Other departments or individuals for whom you produce a product (e.g. a report or some software)	❏	❏
• Other departments to whom you deliver partly finished items on which they will expect to do more work	❏	❏
• Departments or individuals to whom you supply services	❏	❏
• People who look to you for informal guidance or help	❏	❏
• People who are unaware that what you do has an influence on the success of their operations	❏	❏
• Your manager	❏	❏
• Advisory or regulatory groups	❏	❏
• Shareholders or some kind of governing body	❏	❏
• Others _____		

More customers than one might have imagined, perhaps? Anyway, these are the people your operation must do its best to satisfy. Your success, and that of your team and organization, depends on how they feel about what you do for them.

Identifying customer needs

Ask yourself the following questions about each of the customers you identified in checklists on pages 53 and 54.

- Do I know what those customers expect of us?
- How can I be so sure?
- Might they have needs that they don't yet know about themselves?
- What sources of information can I use to find out more, for example:
  - other people in the organization?
  - specialist organizations outside?
  - members of my own team who meet customers?
  - customers themselves (through surveys, questionnaires, focus groups, suggestion boxes, thank-you letters, complaints, re-ordering patterns, and so on)?
- Do all members of my team know as much as they should about our customers' needs?
- How might I ensure that our suppliers (from inside or outside the organization) know as much as they should about what we need on behalf of our customers?
- Do I encourage all concerned to report back on anything they learn about customers' likes and dislikes?
- How can we best keep records of what we have learned about our customers?
- Is there information we collect that we might usefully pass on to other units in the organization to help them satisfy *their* customers?
- And might other departments have information we could get from them to help us satisfy ours?

Meeting customer needs

Then, assuming you have done your best to find out what your customers need, and are continuing to do so, ask yourself:

- Do I and my team make a real effort to look at everything we do as if through our customers' eyes?
- What can I do to ensure that our products or services are *designed* with the customers' needs clearly in mind?
- How can we make sure that what we are offering is clearly and honestly *described* to the customers in terms that they can understand?
- How can I best ensure that my plans and schedules will produce or deliver what we have offered and what the customers are expecting?
- How often do I need to remind my people of how their actions (or lack of action) in the operation might affect customer satisfaction?
- How can I create a work environment that is as conducive as possible to getting the work done properly, through, for example:
  - health and safety factors?
  - equal opportunities aspects?
  - reasonable pay?
  - appropriate equipment?
  - obliging suppliers?
  - adequate resources?
  - contingency plans?
  - accurate, up-to-date records?
- Do I regularly monitor the operation to ensure that the specification is being met (or improved on) from the customers' point of view?
- How can I collect feedback from customers about how well we are meeting their needs?
- What is the best way of taking speedy corrective action if I find that we are not?
- How can I monitor that the corrective action is having the desired effect?
- How can I most productively give feedback to staff about their performance?

- How can I ensure that we always strive to give our customers what they need, rather than what we would find it most easy to provide?

Solving customers' problems

- Are we doing all we can to anticipate problems and help our customers avoid them?
- Despite our best efforts, what kinds of problems (e.g. queries or complaints or special requests) do concern our customers?
- What sort of policy and procedures have we got for dealing with such problems?
- Have we made it clear to customers what these policies and procedures are?
- How do we ensure that our understanding of a customer's problem is the same as the customer's understanding?
- Do I need to consult colleagues elsewhere in the organization before proposing a solution?
- What kind of solution might best meet the needs of the customer without unreasonably penalizing the organization?
- Whose job is it to communicate with the customer and agree a mutually acceptable solution?
- What do we do to ensure that the customer knows exactly how we plan to implement the solution and how long it will take?
- Whose job is it to keep the customer informed of our progress in tackling their problem?
- How shall I monitor the development/delivery of the solution?
- What steps might I take if things don't go as expected?
- How shall I check that the customer is satisfied?
- What records do we need to keep?
- What can we learn from the episode that might prevent such problems arising again or improve our ability to provide a solution if they do? (See **Managing for quality**, page 58)

KEY IDEA

Remember always that our customers can quite probably do without us; but we can't do without them.

Managing for quality

Quality has become a major organizational buzz word in recent years. What people are talking about is providing quality for the *customer*. But they aren't all just *talking* about quality. Many organizations are doing their best to improve it. They have gone beyond the old approach of quality control – inspecting poor quality *out* towards quality *assurance* – designing good quality *in*.

If your organization already has a quality assurance system

	Yes	No
● Do all staff know the organization's policy on quality?	❏	❏
● Have staff been consulted in developing it?	❏	❏
● Were staff suggestions taken into account?	❏	❏
● Have *standards* of quality been clearly laid down?	❏	❏
● Are these reasonable, measurable and achievable?	❏	❏
● Are they clearly related to customers'/clients' satisfaction?	❏	❏
● Have they been made clear to all concerned (e.g. to you)?	❏	❏
● Have the *procedures* needed for quality been identified?	❏	❏
● Have they been made clear to all concerned (e.g. to you)?	❏	❏
● Is there a monitoring system to check that standards are being met and procedures followed?	❏	❏
● Do its findings lead to corrective action being taken?	❏	❏
● Are people rewarded for achieving high quality?	❏	❏

	Yes	No
• Is there a process for monitoring the costs of running the quality assurance system?	❏	❏
• Do the benefits exceed the costs?	❏	❏
• Are enough efforts devoted to finding out what training your staff need to help them maintain quality standards?	❏	❏
• Is adequate training and staff development provided?	❏	❏
• Are staff generally satisfied with the operation of the quality assurance system?	❏	❏

If your organization has no system

1 If your organization does not have an overall quality assurance system, do you have one for your operation?

2 If so, do your team members know what it demands of them individually?

3 If not, consider setting up your own system with the questions in the list above and those below.

4 How can you be sure as you might be about what your customers expect of you by way of a quality product or service? (See the checklists in **Satisfying customer needs**, page 52.)

5 What evidence is there that customers are sometimes less than satisfied with what you provide them with?

6 What kinds of regular failures of quality can you and your team members identify?

7 Are they to do with faults in:
  – objectives ?
  – plans?
  – resources?
  – equipment or materials?
  – attitudes?
  – people's competence?
  – communication?
  – monitoring?

- corrective action?
- others

8   Do you know how to identify the location and causes of quality
    breakdown by means of:
    - brainstorming?
    - interviewing?
    - pareto analysis?
    - fishbone diagrams?
    - flow diagrams?
    - critical path analysis?
    - milestones?
    - control charts?

9   How can you collect suggestions from your staff about how to prevent
    such failures arising?

10 What sort of a system can you set up to close any quality gaps and
    ensure that customers get what they have a right to expect?

11 What briefing or training needs will arise from setting up the new
    system? (Maybe you'll need to consult the checklists on **Managing
    change**, page 88.)

12 How can you publicize your quality assurance scheme and its
    benefits:
    - to reassure customers?
    - to maintain the commitment of your staff?

13 What do you feel you need to learn yourself (e.g. see **8** above) in
    order to set up or work with an effective quality assurance system?

KEY IDEA

A good quality assurance system must satisfy customers rather than
bureaucracy – and it must be workable by staff.

Planning

Planning is an attempt to control the future. Some people just settle for anything the future happens to bring them – 'Whatever will be, will be'. They simply react to it. As a manager you are paid to do otherwise. You need to be *proactive*. That is, you need to think ahead and consider:

(a) how you want things to turn out;

(b) how they might turn out if you take no action – and

(c) what you need to do to make the future as much like (a) as possible.

In short, you need to plan.

Senior managers in an organization may be planning several years ahead – thinking, for instance, of new products and services, of new ways of obtaining resources, and of new ways of structuring the organization. Most of us, however, have a shorter 'time horizon'. Our managerial planning is usually concerned with the next few months or, at most, one or two years into the future. And we usually have to plan within the constraints – of objectives, staffing, time, budgets, etc. – that arise from the plans of more senior managers.

Planning is largely a matter of applied common sense. Much the same thought processes and consultation skills are required in planning how to introduce a new computer system or move to new offices as in planning a family holiday or an extension to your house. A plan has three major aspects:

1 *Objectives:* what are the goals, targets, outcomes or results you intend to accomplish?

2 *Implementation:* how are people and resources to be combined, in what activities over what time period, to accomplish the objectives?

3 *Evaluation:* how is the progress of the implementation to be continuously monitored so that amendments to 1 and 2 can be made if things are not working out as they should?

The checklists in this section are largely concerned with **2** above. For **1**, see the checklists on **Managing with objectives** (page 67), and for **3** see those on **Controlling** (page 71). So try asking yourself the questions that follow in the next few pages.

Do I really need to plan?

	Yes	No
● Can I honestly say that I have no need to plan because:		
– I have few individuals to manage?	❏	❏
– there are few different activities involved?	❏	❏
– it is all routine anyway and will 'run itself'?	❏	❏
– my timescale is very short?	❏	❏
– I can have no influence over how things will turn out?	❏	❏
● If I've answered 'yes' to any of the above questions, am I *quite* sure that some attempt at planning might not improve my managing?	❏	❏
● Are plans prepared for my section by someone else, e.g. by my manager?	❏	❏
● If so, do they leave me no scope for any planning of my own?	❏	❏
● If I've answered 'yes' to both of these questions, might I manage more effectively if I had more influence over the planning for my section?	❏	❏
● If so, how might I obtain such influence? _____		

There will be few managers who really have no need to plan and no influence at all in planning at least some aspects of their section's work. Assuming you will be doing some planning, the following checklists cover the kinds of questions to ask yourself. You can consider them in the order listed – but the planning process could begin with almost any of them. And even after you've answered one of them, you may need to come back to it and reconsider your answer in the light of your answers to later questions.

THE CONTEXT OF PLANNING

The context of planning

	Yes	No
● Are there procedures within the organization, or expectations from my manager, that I must follow in my planning?	❑	❑
● Must my plan(s) take a standard form?	❑	❑
● Do my plans need to fit in with those of other managers?	❑	❑
● Is there a date by which my plan(s) must be ready for discussion with my manager or others?	❑	❑
● If so do I know when it is?	❑	❑
● Do I know with whom I need to consult (e.g. my employees) *before* finalizing my plan(s)?	❑	❑
● Am I aware of how the organization rewards or penalizes managers who plan well or less well?	❑	❑

What goes into the plan?

- For how long a period ahead am I planning?
- What overall goals are we trying to achieve? (See the checklists on **Managing with objectives**, page 67.)
- What sub-goals must we achieve *on the way* to achieving the overall goals?
- Which are the higher and lower priorities among our goals?
- What sort of activities do we need to engage in?
- Will the types and level of activity be constant or will they vary over the period for which I am planning?
- What kind of staffing will be needed to do this work?
- If I do not have adequate staffing at present can I:
  - increase the adequacy of present staff (e.g. by training)? ❑
  - obtain additional competent staff? ❑
  - train new staff in time? ❑

    – modify activities? ❏

    – modify overall goals? ❏

    – others _____

    _____

- If some of my existing staff seem incapable of playing a part in the activities that lie ahead, what am I to do with them?

- What other resources shall I need?

- At what points shall I need them?

The form of the plan

	Yes	No

- Do I need to draw up a 'key events' list – showing the date (or even the hour) by which certain vital events must take place if the plan is to achieve its overall objective? For example, dates by which certain:
  - sub-goals must have been achieved ❏ ❏
  - activities must have been completed ❏ ❏
  - other activities must have been started ❏ ❏
  - targets or deadlines must have been met ❏ ❏

- Can I see how other (less vital) events fit in around such a sequence of key events? ❏ ❏

- Am I committed to 'milestone planning' – i.e. am I expected to report progress at regular intervals? ❏ ❏

- If so what activities do I expect to:
  - be ongoing? _____
  - have already been completed at each of the reporting dates? _____
  - _____

- Do I need to draw up a budget or a 'cash flow' forecast – showing how much money will be paid out and taken in as the plan proceeds? ❏ ❏

- Do I need help (e.g. from accountants) in forecasting cash flow? ❏ ❏

	Yes	No

- Given the difference between the predicted outflow and inflow of cash, can we still afford to proceed with the work as planned? ❑ ❑

- Will it be helpful/vital to me and/or others to present the plan in the form of:
  - a list? ❑ ❑
  - a table? ❑ ❑
  - a bar chart (or Gantt chart)? ❑ ❑
  - a network diagram? ❑ ❑
  - a budget? (see **Managing finance**, page 103) ❑ ❑

- From whom can I get help with any of the above techniques or jargon? _____

Analyzing the plan

	Yes	No

- Can I see any potential overruns, bottlenecks and snarl-ups in the plan? ❑ ❑

- If so, can I see ways to guard against such problems occurring? ❑ ❑

- Shall I prepare contingency plans to put into operation if problems do nevertheless occur? ❑ ❑

- Are there low-priority aspects of the plan that can be jettisoned to safeguard more important aspects? ❑ ❑

- Can I identify areas of my plan where lack of information has forced me to make 'guestimates' about time, resources, etc? ❑ ❑

- If so, can I see how I might obtain better information as the plan proceeds? ❑ ❑

- Is it possible that new *opportunities* may arise during the operation of the plan? ❑ ❑

	Yes	No
● Will I be able to revise the plan so as to take advantage of any such opportunities?	❏	❏
● Can I keep the plan as *flexible* as possible by:		
– mentally allowing for some activities to take rather longer than the plan indicates?	❏	❏
– having money or resources up my sleeve in case of emergencies or unmissable opportunities?	❏	❏
– avoiding scheduling too many key events or crucial activities to happen at the same time?	❏	❏
– encouraging my staff to report emerging problems or opportunities before it is too late to take the most appropriate action?	❏	❏
– building in alternative courses of action to meet foreseeable problems or opportunities?	❏	❏
– regularly updating the plan in the light of new information?	❏	❏
– being brave enough to change my mind and/or admit that some aspects of my initial plan were deficient?	❏	❏
– others _____		
● Can I see how to monitor the progress of the plan and control the work? (See the checklists on **Controlling**, page 71 and **Managing finance**, page 103.)	❏	❏

Communicating about the plan

	Yes	No
● In drawing up the plan, have I consulted everyone I should within my own team?	❏	❏
● Have I consulted all necessary outsiders as well?	❏	❏
● Does the plan fit in with other people's plans?	❏	❏
● Has the plan been fully understood and agreed by everyone whose co-operation I need?	❏	❏

	Yes	No
● Can I make sure that all concerned know about the total plan (not just their bits) – e.g. with a wall chart?	❏	❏
● And can I keep them informed of progress – e.g. with a regularly updated newsletter or e-mail?	❏	❏

> **KEY IDEA**
>
> Always have a plan – but be prepared to change it in the light of new information.

Managing with objectives

'Managing by objectives' was once a management fad. Like most new approaches, it was oversold. Nevertheless while the slogan faded, the approach left its mark. Most of us have come to accept that defining our objectives clearly can help us manage more effectively.

Objectives should state as specifically as possible what an individual or group is expected to have achieved by the end of a certain period. They should be phrased in such a way that it will be clear whether or not they have been achieved – or at least the extent to which they have been achieved. Ideally they should be expressed in terms of measurable quantities – for example:

- reduce absenteeism by at least 50 per cent by the end of the year; or
- get all your staff trained to the new standard by Easter; or
- ensure that each branch has been visited at least three times during the year; or
- circulate final draft of a report at least two weeks before the next meeting.

Notice that these statements refer to *products* or *results*. They indicate aims, targets, goals or deadlines. They refer not to people's activities but to the expected *outcomes* of those activities.

Objectives remind you of where you are going. If we don't know where we are going, we are liable to land up somewhere we'd rather not be. They help you explain what your section is trying to accomplish and how its activities fit in with the work of the organization. (See the checklists on **Planning**, page 60.)

Just as importantly they can act as performance indicators – in two ways:

- They can help you monitor the work of your team – and take corrective action where important objectives are not being achieved, or where new ones need to be introduced.

- They can help you weigh up the performance of each individual within your team – and praise, admonish, offer extra help or whatever seems appropriate.

Do you have any objectives?

	Yes	No
Can you state what your manager's objectives are for the next few months or so?	❏	❏
Have you agreed with your manager any objectives that you (with your team) should be aiming towards?	❏	❏
Can you see how your objectives (if any) relate to your manager's objectives (if any)?	❏	❏
Do you have any objectives that have *not* been agreed with your manager?	❏	❏
Does each member of your team have objectives?	❏	❏
If so, has each one understood and agreed these objectives?	❏	❏
If you don't have objectives at present, do you have any difficulties appraising the work performance of your staff?	❏	❏
And does your manager make sensible appraisals of *your* work?	❏	❏
Are you satisfied that the practices reflected in the answers you've given above are helpful to your effectiveness as a manager?	❏	❏

● What changes might improve matters? _____

_____

Starting to set objectives

When you are developing objectives for your team, or discussing your own objectives with your manager, here are some initial points to consider.

● In which aspects of your work would objectives be helpful?
  – Volume of activity ❑
  – Quality standards ❑
  – Productivity ❑
  – Profits ❑
  – Costs ❑
  – Meeting of targets/deadlines ❑
  – Safety ❑
  – Development of new products or services ❑
  – Customer/client satisfaction ❑
  – New customers/clients ❑
  – Morale within the team ❑
  – Relations with other groups in the organization ❑
  – Other aspects _____

● For how far ahead (e.g. one month or one year) is it necessary/sensible to set certain objectives?

● How can we state our objectives so that their attainment can be *verified*? (e.g. what evidence might convince us that customer satisfaction had improved?)

● More specifically, to what extent can our objectives be stated in *measurable* terms (e.g. a reduction of at least 20 per cent in customer complaints by the end of the year?)

● But do they avoid *arbitrary* quantification (e.g. stipulating a 20 per cent reduction when there are no grounds for thinking this is any more or less attainable than a 50 per cent or 100 per cent reduction)?

- If the degree of attainment of some objectives (e.g. improvement of department morale) has to be partly a matter of *opinion*, whose opinions will be taken into account – mine only, my manager's, the members of the department, etc?
- How will such opinions be weighed against one another?
- Can some of our objectives usefully be broken down into *sub*-objectives – i.e. goals that must be attained *on the way* if the overall objective is to be attained?

How do the objectives suit your team?

	Yes	No
• Are the objectives realistically attainable?	❏	❏
• Are they sufficiently challenging ('stretching') for the individuals concerned?	❏	❏
• Do they take into account the career development (e.g. training) needs of individuals as well as the need to get a job done?	❏	❏
• Is it clear to me and to the team how each person's objectives fit in with those of the others and how all relate to those of the organization?	❏	❏
• Do all members of the team know how the objectives will be *used* – for planning, monitoring, making adjustments to workplans, appraising their performance and so on?	❏	❏
• What will be lost – by me, the team or the organization – if some of the objectives are *not* attained?	❏	❏
• What rewards, if any, will be forthcoming if they *are* attained?	❏	❏
• Does each member of the team fully understand and accept his or her objectives?	❏	❏
• Shall I ensure that each member of the team has a sheet of paper listing his or her objectives?	❏	❏

	Yes	No
● Should I ensure that each member is kept aware of every other member's objectives (including mine) – by putting an overall list on public display?	❏	❏
● How might we most usefully publicize (or even celebrate) the attainment of key objectives? _____		

_____

_____

KEY IDEA

Objectives must not be a straitjacket. Be prepared to review and modify them periodically – and to introduce new ones as necessary.

Controlling

Controlling is the core of a manager's work. Unfortunately the word has unpleasant overtones for many people. They think of Big Brother watching them, of being kept down and of being denied any personal initiative.

To the manager the word means nothing of the sort. What you are controlling is not people but the operations – projects, events and activities – in which your people are involved. In this role you are more like the controls on your central heating system which switch it on or off at various set times or according to temperature. Better still, compare yourself with the pilot of an aircraft, constantly monitoring instruments and outside conditions to make whatever adjustments are necessary to keep on course and arrive safely at the planned destination.

Notice the use, in the last sentence, of the words 'monitoring', 'adjustments' and 'planned'. What you need to do, as a manager, to keep in control is to:

1 *Have a plan* that includes goals (objectives, standards, targets, deadlines) you are trying to attain.

2 *Monitor* your team's work – to collect 'feedback' as to how things are going.

3 *Compare* how things are going with how they should be going if the plan is to be attained.

4 *Recognize* areas where performance is below standard or where new opportunities have arisen.

5 *Act* to remedy the shortfall or to make the most of new opportunities.

Of the five items above, **1** is dealt with in our checklists on **Managing with objectives** (page 67), **Planning** (page 60) and **Managing finance** (page 103). Item **5** is covered under **Decision-making** (page 76). So the checklists that follow are chiefly concerned with items **2, 3** and **4** – monitoring what is actually happening, comparing the actual with the intended and recognizing matters that call for you to take action.

What do I need to monitor?

- What you need to monitor will depend on what you are expecting from your team. If you have a clearly defined plan you should have no trouble identifying the key factors you need to keep an eye on. Which of the following do *you* most need to monitor?
    - Achievement of output targets ❑
    - Meeting of deadlines ❑
    - Quality of products/services ❑
    - Standards of performance ❑
    - Equal opportunities ❑
    - Staff morale ❑
    - Cost effectiveness ❑
    - Others _____

- Which of these aspects of your team's work might you need information about in order to monitor how things are going?
    - Amounts produced ❑
    - Number of customers dealt with ❑
    - Speed of response to demands ❑
    - Sales ❑

- Levels of stocks ❑
- Profits made ❑
- Customer/client response ❑
- Interpersonal relationships within the team ❑
- Relationships with the rest of the organization ❑
- Relationships with people outside ❑
- Resources used ❑
- Use of materials ❑
- Use of equipment ❑
- Others _____

	Yes	No
● Do you at present 'manage by exception' – relying on the ability and willingness of your staff to identify and bring to your attention only those differences between what was planned and what is happening that demand your personal attention?	❑	❑
● If not, does it sound like an effective way of managing in your situation?	❑	❑
● If so, can you see how you might arrange your control system so as to manage by exception?	❑	❑

● What is the main thing you would need to do? _____

How to gather information

Basically, there are two ways to gather the kinds of feedback you need to monitor your team's work. These might be called the *systematic* and the *casual*, or the formal and the informal, or the routine and the occasional. Both have a part to play. You need to be sure that information is gathered formally and systematically, as a matter of routine. But you also need to keep your eyes and ears open for things of relevance that will just happen to come to your attention. Tick any in the two lists overleaf that may be useful sources of control data for you.

Systematic, formal, routine data

- Records kept by staff (e.g. a sales rep's log) ❑
- Weekly or other regular reports from staff ❑
- Statistics you compile yourself ❑
- Regular reports you prepare for your manager ❑
- Routine statistics (e.g. on production or sales) sent to
  you from another department ❑
- Reports on your expenditure against budget sent to you
  by the accountants ❑
- Others _____

_____

N.B. When setting up a system for collecting control data, make sure you don't demand information just for the sake of it – information that never has any bearing on your decisions. There are times when too much information is just as counter-productive as too little.

Casual, informal, occasional data

- What you see of your staff performing their tasks ❑
- What you see of the workplace or of the materials/
  equipment being used ❑
- Unusual incidents ❑
- Conversations/discussions with your staff ❑
- Questioning of staff ❑
- Overheard discussions/rows among staff ❑
- Comments from other managers or their staff ❑
- Customer/client comments ❑
- Your gut feeling about how things are going ❑
- Other data _____

_____

N.B. Don't rely on routine data alone. Especially if it comes from outside your section, it may be too late to be very helpful. Keep alert for the casual data that may allow you to take control measures early – before things get messy, painful and expensive to put right.

What can be done?

The feedback you get from your control data (formal or informal) allows you to compare what is happening with what you planned. If there is a discrepancy, you may need to do something about it. Here are some questions you may have to ask yourself.

	Yes	No
● Is the discrepancy big enough to be worth doing something about?	❏	❏
● If so, can I discover the *cause* of the discrepancy?	❏	❏
● Is it enough to correct the discrepancy or must I also cure the cause?	❏	❏
● Do I need to reset any of our goals/objectives/ targets/ deadlines/budgets because:		
– outside circumstances have made them unrealistic?	❏	❏
– I was over-optimistic in the first place?	❏	❏
– team members have not tried hard enough?	❏	❏
– staff have lacked necessary abilities or support?	❏	❏
– some staff are too perfectionist?	❏	❏
– I have not managed as well as I should?	❏	❏
– certain goals are no longer worth attaining?	❏	❏
– new goals have emerged that are even more worth attaining (given that our resources are limited)?	❏	❏
– others _____		
● If so, can I reset any of our goals *without*:		
– removing my staff's incentive to get as close as possible to the goals?	❏	❏
– disenchanting staff who have tried extra hard?	❏	❏
– undermining efforts towards other ongoing goals?	❏	❏
– making staff cynical about future goal-setting?	❏	❏
– setting another unattainable goal?	❏	❏
– creating difficulties elsewhere in the section or in the wider organization?	❏	❏

	Yes	No
– undermining my credibility (with my staff and my manager and/or with other managers)?	❏	❏
● Do I need to improve my team's standard of performance or productivity by:		
– communicating more clearly or more often?	❏	❏
– agreeing new rules and procedures?	❏	❏
– ensuring more carefully that goals and procedures are understood and agreed?	❏	❏
– setting up a better feedback control system?	❏	❏
– providing better incentives?	❏	❏
– cajoling, persuading or bribing?	❏	❏
– coaching and training?	❏	❏
– somewhat increasing the pressure?	❏	❏
– advising against overfussy perfectionism?	❏	❏
– having discussions with poor performers?	❏	❏
– taking formal disciplinary action?	❏	❏
– getting rid of some individuals?	❏	❏
– taking on some new kinds of staff?	❏	❏
– improving relationships with other parts of the organization?	❏	❏
– being more on the ball myself (especially in planning and controlling)?	❏	❏
– Others _____		

KEY IDEA

Make sure you set up a control system – but don't let it be so elaborate and time-consuming that it uses up more resources than it saves.

Decision-making

Decision-making is one of the things you will do most frequently as a manager. It is what you do in response to problems. And by problems I mean not just difficulties, but also puzzles, challenges and any situations that seem to need something doing about them.

As a manager you will be faced with a stream of such problems and it is your job to solve them. Your problems will be of many kinds. They may centre on technical matters or on human relations, on financial questions or on the 'politics' of your organization, and so on. Some will be threatening while others – like how to respond to a new market that has unexpectedly opened up – will offer you exciting opportunities. Some will be trivial, others of momentous importance to the organization. In all cases, however, the appropriateness of the decisions you make is a measure of your effectiveness as a manager.

Put simply there are just four steps in problem-solving.

1. Identify what the problem is.

2. Decide how to solve it.

3. Apply the solution.

4.   Check that the solution has worked.

But there are plenty of snags in such a process. For example:

- the problem you identify may be hiding an even more serious one that goes undetected;
- there may be several possible solutions that are difficult to choose from;
- solving one problem can create more problems;
- some problems have no entirely satisfactory solution;
- you may not have the time and resources to develop or implement the ideal solution;
- thinking about 'solving' problems may prevent you seeing them more positively as challenges and opportunities.

There are many approaches to problem-solving. Some are more systematic and reliable than others. You can decide which are most useful to you from the checklists that follow.

Quick and/or dirty approaches

Which of the following approaches do you sometimes take when faced with a decision to make?

- Pass it on to my manager ❏
- Get some group to take responsibility for it ❏
- Try whatever occurs to me first and then think again if it doesn't work out ❏
- Choose whatever solution is urged upon me by my most powerful colleague ❏
- Adopt whatever solution was used last time a similar problem arose ❏
- Do whatever will cost least and/or cause least fuss ❏
- Find out what sort of decision my manager wants ❏
- Choose whatever solution I can most easily understand ❏
- Put off the decision in the hope that the problem will go away ❏
- Hope that a solution will emerge by itself, given enough time ❏

We all use such approaches now and again – especially when we face confused situations and don't have time to sort them out. It's called 'muddling through'. We sometimes get away with it. But there are more systematic ways of setting about decision-making.

Rational decision-making

Many management trainers recommend some type of rational approach to decision-making. By this, they mean putting in rather more thought than goes into the approaches listed above. If you follow a rational approach to decision-making you will be logical and systematic, taking every relevant factor into account and giving due weight to all possibilities.

Here are the questions to ask yourself in pursuing such an approach. I have arranged them in what seems like a practical sequence. But remember that you may often need to retrace your steps when struggling with a problem and reconsider questions that you answered earlier, or even ignored as not being very relevant.

Defining the problem

Too many managers launch into tackling the wrong problem. Here are some questions to think about that may save you from wasting your time on wild goose chases.

	Yes	No
● What kind of decision is required?		
– Technical	❑	❑
– Human	❑	❑
– Financial	❑	❑
– Political	❑	❑
– Others _____		
_____		
● Why has the need for a decision arisen? _____		
_____		
● What appears to be the problem? _____		
_____		
● Does it:		
– pose a threat?	❑	❑
– or offer an opportunity?	❑	❑
● Has such a problem been faced before?	❑	❑
● If so, was it solved?	❑	❑
● Is the problem a symptom of some *deeper* problem?	❑	❑
● If so, does the deeper problem need dealing with also (perhaps first)?	❑	❑
● Is the problem one of a related *set* of problems?	❑	❑
● If so, can it be solved without tackling the others at the same time?	❑	❑

- What additional information do I need to be sure I've identified all relevant factors? For instance:
  - Who or what is involved in the problem? _____
  _____
  - Where is the problem? _____
  _____
  - How big is the problem? _____
  _____
  - When did the problem begin? _____
  _____
  - How often is the problem occurring? _____
  _____
  - Other factors _____
  _____

Deciding how to deal with the problem

A few more questions to save you from hasty action that you might live to regret.

	Yes	No
● Does the problem really come within my area of responsibility?	❏	❏
● Would it matter if the problem remained unsolved?	❏	❏
● Do different people in my team (or elsewhere) feel differently about the problem?	❏	❏
● If so, which and how? _____ _____		
● Should I/must I share the decision-making with other people?	❏	❏
● If so, which? _____ _____		
● Do I need to delegate it to one or more of my staff?	❏	❏
● If so, which? _____ _____		

- How much priority shall I give the problem (compared with other things I ought to be doing)? _____

	Yes	No
● Do I need to go for:		
– a once-and-for-all solution?	❑	❑
– or will a temporary solution be OK?	❑	❑

- How much time, money and resources can I spend in developing a solution? _____

- Is there any off-the-shelf solution that has been used in similar cases before and that I can consider adopting/ adapting? ❑ ❑

- Who besides me must be satisfied with the solution? _____

- Which special expectations or objectives within my section and/or within the organization as a whole must the solution take into account? _____

- On what grounds might different people criticize any solution I might come up with? _____

- What *criteria of acceptability* (to me and to others) must my solution meet? _____

- How would I rank those criteria in order of importance? _____

Generating possible solutions

Now for some questions that may enable you to come up with a *variety* of possible solutions. The aim is to let your mind 'hang loose' and roam pro-ductively beyond the *first* solution that happens to come to you.

	Yes	No

- Can I force myself to produce several possible solutions before I start criticizing any of them? ☐ ☐

- Can I usefully make analogies between my problem and problems in other walks of life – sport, music, family life, etc? ☐ ☐

- Can I generate 'fantasy' solutions that may nevertheless contain *some* elements that can contribute to the eventual solution? For example, by:
  - looking at the problem from a different angle? ☐
  - redefining the problem? ☐
  - asking how to solve the opposite problem? ☐
  - exaggerating the problem? ☐
  - asking how some famous or fictional person might have tackled it? ☐
  - imagining that certain of the practical constraints need no longer apply? ☐ ☐
  - transporting the problem to some far-fetched situation like being cast away on a deserted island or going back in time? ☐ ☐

- Are there older or wiser colleagues I can go to for ideas? ☐ ☐

- Do I need ideas from anyone *outside* the organization? ☐ ☐

- Can I get colleagues involved in a brainstorming exercise in which we creatively spark off one another's ideas without interrupting the flow by criticizing or evaluating? ☐ ☐

- Can I accept that the wildest of ideas may eventually contribute to a practicable solution? ☐ ☐

Evaluating possible solutions

These questions should help you choose the most appropriate solution as rationally as possible.

- Can I use any of the approaches to **Evaluating proposed changes** mentioned in the checklists on **Managing change**, page 91? _____

- Which possible solutions look worth considering further? _____

  _____

- What would be the benefits of adopting each solution? _____

  _____

- What would be the costs in time or money? _____

  _____

- What further problems might each solution give rise to?

  _____

- How satisfactory might each solution be if circumstances changed in
  various foreseeable ways? _____

  _____

- For which solutions do the pros outweigh the cons? _____

  _____

- If none of the alternatives seems outstandingly good, which one seems
  least bad? _____

  _____

- Which solution best meets the *criteria of acceptability* developed on
  page 81? _____

  _____

Evaluating your decision

Finally, some questions about what happens next:

- What effect will my decision have on other people? _____

  _____

- Who will help implement the decision? _____

  _____

- Who needs to be told what? _____

  _____

- How must I tell them:
  - face-to-face?   ❏
  - on the telephone?   ❏

– in writing? ❏

– through another person? ❏

● When must they be told? _____

_____

● Is there need for:

– retraining? ❏

– updating? ❏

Yes No

● Might there be resistance? (If so, see the checklists on
Managing change, page 88.) ❏ ❏

● What do I need to do to *monitor* the results of the
decision – so that I can modify it, if necessary? _____

_____

Decision-making is not an activity separate from all other managerial activities. Most of the other activities described in this book will necessarily involve you in making decisions – e.g. about how to plan a new project or how to motivate your staff. Some decisions will be tougher to make than others and some will have bigger risks attached to them. But you will be making decisions of one kind or another every day of your working life as a manager.

KEY IDEA

Always aim to take a rational approach – but don't spend so long on it that you make the right decision too late.

Managing equal opportunities

Managing equal opportunities is about treating people *fairly* – and ensuring that your team members do also. Many people are prejudiced about people from other groups – e.g. people of another sex, race or religion or people who are gay, who have a disability or who are older or younger than they are. Usually, though not always, they are prejudiced in a negative way. That is, they believe that all members of such a group share certain undesirable characteristics. Or maybe they simply think they are inferior or lack certain abilities.

So, when prejudiced people meet an individual from such a group, they close their eyes to that person as a person. They take it for granted that he or she is typical of what they think the group is like, and is therefore unworthy or inferior or incapable. If they *act* on this assumption, they are treating that person unfairly – differently than they would a person from a group they feel more positive about. They are then discriminating against that person.

If such discrimination happens in your team it may:

- prevent individuals getting the life-chances they deserve;
- limit the potential productivity of your operation;
- give your section a poor image in the organization;
- give your organization a poor image in the outside world;
- offend against your organization's equal opportunities policy;
- break the law.

Maybe you've had experience yourself of being treated unfairly for no good reason – not because of what you are as an individual or what you've done, but simply because you are of a particular sex, race, religion, etc. If so, you'll be in a good position to empathize with other people who are treated unfairly. Perhaps you'll need to help members of your team to do likewise.

Preparing for equal opportunities

- Ensure that you understand your organization's equal opportunities policy and what it demands of you as a manager.
- If you get the opportunity, offer your suggestions as to how that policy might be improved or carried out.
- Ensure that all your staff:
  - are also aware of the equal opportunities policy and have a chance to discuss it with you;
  - know what will be regarded as unacceptable speech and behaviour and provision of facilities, and why it is unacceptable;
  - know what is likely to happen to them if they violate the organization's equal opportunities policy.

- Provide your staff with a chance to discuss examples of the following:
  - language offensive to members of certain groups;
  - language that needlessly excludes members of certain groups;
  - offensive objects (e.g. sexist pin-up and racist posters);
  - jokes made at the expense of other groups;
  - sexual harassment;
  - work environments that are needlessly difficult (or impossible) for people with certain disabilities;
  - working practices that are needlessly difficult (or impossible) for people of certain religions;
  - stereotyping;
  - actions that are directly discriminatory;
  - actions that discriminate indirectly (e.g. needlessly setting a height limit for job candidates that would unintentionally rule out many otherwise suitable candidates whose ethnic origins are the Indian subcontinent or southeast Asia);

- Try to identify any people connected with the organization (or people who might be connected with it but for discrimination) who are being denied opportunities because staff members discriminate against them. For example:
  - employees who are being denied promotion or other rewards;
  - potential employees who don't get appointed;
  - customers or clients who don't get the best products or service;
  - potential customers who are discouraged from asking;
  - suppliers who are treated less favourably than others;
  - others _____

  _____

- If you do identify such people, ask them to give you examples of their unfair treatment and get their suggestions as to how matters might be improved.

- Look for ways of enabling members of your team to see such unfair treatment through the eyes of the people who receive it.

- Consider taking what is called 'positive action' to help groups who have previously been discriminated against to improve their position, e.g. through special encouragement, training or new facilities. (But don't get tempted into positive discrimination, e.g. a quota system, because it is still discrimination and, in the UK, it is illegal.)

- Consider developing an action plan for improving your section's performance on equal opportunities – with targets and deadlines for overcoming specified forms of unfairness where appropriate.

- Agree the action plan with your team and ensure that each member has a copy of it.

- Brief each member of your staff about how they are expected to contribute to making the action plan work.

- Provide appropriate training to help them develop the understanding, awareness and sensitivity to do so.

- Monitor the progress of your plan by keeping records of equal opportunities issues that arise in your operation and by measuring progress against any targets and deadlines you may have agreed.

Applying equal opportunities policy

- Are you already aware of ways in which one or more members of your staff may be acting in discriminatory ways. For example, towards:
  - women? ☐
  - people from certain ethnic groups? ☐
  - people of certain religions? ☐
  - people in certain age groups? ☐
  - people with a disability? ☐
  - gay people? ☐
  - people of another nationality? ☐
  - people of another profession/trade? ☐
  - others _____

- Have you considered possible discrimination against:
  - fellow team members? ☐

- – people elsewhere in the organization? ❑
- – suppliers? ❑
- – customers or clients? ❑
- – others

- Have you considered, for example:
  - – the language team members use *about* other people? ❑
  - – the things they say *to* other people? ❑
  - – the 'body language' they display towards them? ❑
  - – the things they do to them (e.g. 'practical jokes')? ❑
  - – how they work with them (or resist doing so)? ❑
  - – how they deal with their requests for help? ❑
  - – how they allocate them to tasks? ❑
  - – how they give them feedback or criticism? ❑
  - – how they hire or fire them? ❑
  - – what working facilities they provide? ❑
  - – others _____

If you find that someone is behaving in a discriminatory way, let the person know that you have noticed, tell them why it is undesirable and what will happen if they do it again. If they continue with their discriminatory behaviour, start disciplinary procedure. (See the checklists on **Disciplining staff**, page 173.)

If your organization has someone responsible for equal opportunities, keep them informed of the case. Consider whether you need to learn more yourself about the practical and legal issues surrounding equal opportunities, discrimination and fair working practices.

> **KEY IDEA**
>
> Discrimination is rooted in prejudice, and people have strong feelings about their prejudices. If your goal is to overcome them, look out for conflict!

Managing change

Modern organizations are never static for long. Neither the local primary school, the country-wide chain of retail stores nor the multinational corporation can shelter from the winds of change that are constantly blowing, soft or strong. For the manager, change is a fact of life. Sometimes you will be introducing changes yourself; at other times you have them thrust upon you by your managers – or by the actions of other departments. Whether it's just that new equipment is needed in the warehouse, or that head office has introduced a new accounting procedure, you will need to plan for and cope with the effects and repercussions.

New laws, new technologies, new consumer demands, new competition – these are among the many reasons why organizations must change. Otherwise they will flounder and perish. Some people relish change. Others fear or resent it. Which way we feel usually depends on whether we have helped initiate the change ourselves or have had it forced upon us.

To be an effective manager of change you will need to recognize when change is desirable, or at least inevitable. You will then need to bring your team to recognize that they will get more benefit by helping decide the precise details of the change than by trying to resist it. This is often easier said than done – especially if you are not too happy about the change yourself. (To plan for changes within your own career, you may like to consult the checklists on **Keeping up to date**, page 267.)

How do you rate as a 'change agent'?

What will be your own strengths and weaknesses in trying to implement change within your organization? To be a successful agent of change you will need to be able to say 'yes' to as many as possible of the first set of questions, and 'no' to as many as possible of the second set.

Advantages

	Yes	No
• Do you understand your organization – who has the power, how the networks operate, where the barriers are?	❏	❏
• Do you speak the organization's language – its special jargon, in-jokes, etc.?	❏	❏

	Yes	No
● Do you understand the local ways of doing things and behaving, and can you act in accordance with the organization's unwritten rules?	❏	❏
● Are you a familiar and non-threatening figure to your colleagues?	❏	❏
● Do you feel that your personal and professional satisfaction is dependent on the organization prospering?	❏	❏
● Do you believe that change usually brings more gains than losses?	❏	❏
● Do you actively look for ways of improving things?	❏	❏

Disadvantages

	Yes	No
● Are you too involved with your section to see the organization as a whole and without bias?	❏	❏
● Might people's expectations of you in your present role conflict with your efforts to work with them towards implementing change?	❏	❏
● Do you have no prior experience of introducing changes?	❏	❏
● Do your other duties leave you insufficient time and energy to think about change?	❏	❏
● Do you feel you are too insecure to guard against challenges from other members of staff?	❏	❏
● Might your past successes or failures prejudice people against you?	❏	❏
● Do you believe that change usually brings more losses than gains?	❏	❏
● Are you inclined to be suspicious of new practices?	❏	❏

Evaluating proposed changes

Sometimes changes will be urged upon you by other people. In such cases, you may need to evaluate the proposal, suggest amendments, or perhaps even oppose it. Here are some useful questions to ask.

	Yes	No
● Are we already doing it?	❑	❑
● Has it been tried unsuccessfully in the past?	❑	❑
● Could it work?	❑	❑
● Is it practical?	❑	❑
● Is it ethical?	❑	❑
● Is it based on empire-building and self-interest?	❑	❑
● Is it based on untested theory or speculation?	❑	❑
● Is it based on fashion or someone's whim?	❑	❑
● Will it solve the problems?	❑	❑
● Might it create more problems than it solves?	❑	❑
● Are the risks acceptable?	❑	❑
● Is it likely to be cost-effective?	❑	❑
● Is it within the existing budget?	❑	❑
● Will it antagonize staff/customers/unions, etc?	❑	❑
● Are the projected improvements in productivity and/or the quality of working life sufficiently *specific* for us to be able to agree on the extent to which they do get attained?	❑	❑
● On balance shall I support the proposed change (with or without suggesting amendments)?	❑	❑
● Or shall I oppose it?	❑	❑
● If I feel I must oppose it, how and with whose support shall I prepare and present the case against it?	❑	❑

N.B. You will, of course, be just as critical in applying such questions to changes you think up yourself as to those proposed by other people.

Preparing for change

Assuming that you personally are ready to foster change within your operation, here are some important questions to ask.

- How can I keep my team members alert to the possible needs for change within our operation?
- How can I promote a *positive* attitude towards change among my team members?
- How can I best explain the basic problem or opportunity that seems to call for a change to be made?
- How, specifically, can I outline the improvements in productivity and/or the quality of working life that we can expect?
- How can I deal with anxieties that the benefits of the change may not outweigh the costs, e.g. in time, money, effort, disruption, etc.?
- How can I make sure my section gets the best possible results from a change I am not 100 per cent convinced about myself?
- How can I change things as little as possible in order to bring about the desired improvement?
- What are the forces or factors that seem to make change necessary or will help it to get established?
- What are the forces or factors that may make the change difficult to implement?
- What problems and side effects are likely to be produced in trying to change?

Planning the change

- With whom do I need to liaise in planning the change?
- Who else is likely to be affected by the change?
- Can they work with me in planning the change?
- How much freedom have we to decide:
  - what needs to be done?

- – in what order?
- – by what target dates?
- – by whom?
- How much time and resources are needed (allowing for any temporarily reduced productivity) in order:
  - – to introduce the change?
  - – to maintain it?
- How can I draw up a realistic timetable for implementing the change – from planning to routine operation?
- How much support will I get from my manager and from top management generally?
- How shall I monitor whether the change is getting established satisfactorily, e.g. formal reports and/or informal observations?
- What early warning system shall I set up to detect:
  - – difficulties?
  - – discontent?
  - – shortages?
  - – delays?
  - – confusions?
  - – unexpected snags, and so on?
- Can I keep a 'fire-fighting' reserve of time and resources to deal with problems whose nature and timing I cannot anticipate?
- Am I alert to modifying the change where experience suggests improvements are necessary?

Overcoming resistance

- Who is likely to be resistant to the change and why?
- Are there any potential resisters within my own team or department?
- Is the change likely to interfere with or have repercussions for the work of other departments and so create resisters elsewhere?
- Are the potential resisters clear about what are expected to be the benefits of the change?

- Am I being honest with them about any particular benefits I would hope to gain personally from the change?
- Do the potential resisters understand how their opposition would affect the people expected to benefit from the change?
- Do they realize the strength of my own personal disappointment (and hopefully feel uncomfortable about it)?
- Who are the opinion leaders among the resisters?
- What are the reasons for their resistance?
- Is there any 'hidden agenda' of objections which the resisters are unwilling to discuss openly, or even admit to?
- If so, how can I best make clear that I am taking such unstated objections into account?
- Are there any aspects of the change about which I and the resisters can agree?
- Do I accept that the change may have some drawbacks I have not yet recognized?
- Are the resisters willing to contribute to the change by suggesting modifications?
- Can I persuade them to convert emotional opposition into practical suggestions?
- Can I convince them of my willingness to make justifiable modifications in line with their suggestions?
- Shall I manage to be even tempered at all times and avoid getting into slanging matches with resisters?
- Can I ensure that respected *supporters* of the chain are present at any important discussion where resisters are likely to be expressing dissent?
- Can I get such respected supporters to lobby the dissenters individually and in private?
- If all else fails, can I:
  - buy off the resisters by giving them something they want; or
  - coerce them by threatening them with the loss of something they already have?

> **KEY IDEA**
>
> Resistance may develop after the change has been introduced, even though it was not evident beforehand.

Developing leadership

If your operation is to run successfully, you will need to work through other people – your team. Furthermore, you will need to give them effective leadership.

What is leadership? Most of us believe we can recognize it when we meet it. We may even believe that we can tell the difference between good leadership and poor leadership. But it is very difficult to define.

My tip would be to think of leadership as being the management of *people* – just as we might think of administration as being the management of other resources (money and materials). Thus, as a manager your job is to achieve results through other people, with the aid of various resources. In short, you need to be both administrator and leader.

What then, makes an effective leader? How does one develop oneself as a leader? Various theories have developed over the years. The most important point to emerge is that there is no one way of being an effective leader. To be an effective leader you have to be capable of behaving differently in different circumstances.

In particular, you need to decide which of these three basic styles is most appropriate:

- **Directive**: where you tell your staff what to do.
- **Consultative**: where you encourage your staff to involve themselves in your decision-making.
- **Delegatory**: where you expect your staff to do a certain amount of the decision-making themselves.

You can imagine a scale running all the way through from very directive ('bossy') at one end to very delegatory at the other – with consultative leadership lying somewhere in the middle. You can be more or less directive;

more or less consultative; more or less delegatory. You should be able to choose a leadership style that fits in with:

- what you can feel comfortable with;
- what your staff can feel comfortable with;
- what each particular task demands and;
- what the organization allows.

The following checklists will help you choose appropriately. They will also remind you of other factors that will aid you in getting the kind of co-operation you want from your staff. (You may also find it useful to look at the checklists on **Delegating**, page 16.)

Do you have a preferred approach?

The following list indicates several different approaches to leadership. Tick any you *have used* at some time or other. Is there any one that you would *prefer* to use more than others? If so, circle its box.

(a) *Telling* – I decide what to do and simply tell my staff to do it ❑

(b) *Selling* – I decide what to do but then I explain to my staff why it needs to be done ❑

(c) *Fine-tuning* – I decide what to do but I invite questions and comments from staff in case this reveals ways I can improve my decision ❑

(d) *Consulting* – I present staff with one or more tentative solutions to a problem and invite discussion of them before I make the final decision ❑

(e) *Problem-solving* – I present staff with the problem and get them to come up with possible solutions before I make the decision ❑

(f) *Partly delegating* – I present staff with the problem and let them make the decision ❑

(g) *Fully delegating* – I expect staff to both define the
problem and decide what to do about it (subject to
whatever limits I must impose) ❑

Clearly the further you come down the scale above, the less you are exert-
ing your own authority, and the greater the freedom you are giving your
staff. None of these approaches is necessarily more right than any other.
The most appropriate approach depends on factors in you, in the people you
are leading, in the nature of the task and in the organization you are working for.

Factors in you

Think about each of the following factors in your own make up. Each of
them might lead you towards one or other of the seven approaches (a–g.)
Circle your most likely approach for each factor.

- Any basic belief you may have about the extent to
  which a manager should be seen to be in charge or
  that staff should be expected to contribute to
  decision-making   a b c d e f g

- Your personal preference for taking sole responsibility
  for all decisions that affect you as opposed to sharing
  this responsibility with others   a b c d e f g

- How far you feel you can trust your staff to make
  sensible and responsible decisions   a b c d e f g

- How strongly you feel that you know better than
  anyone else what needs to be done   a b c d e f g

- The amount of credibility you have with your staff as
  someone who can make decisions that are in their
  best interests   a b c d e f g

- The extent to which you can live with the risk or
  uncertainty of giving up some of your control   a b c d e f g

- How you feel when you are working under unusual
  pressure, resulting in stress   a b c d e f g

If you find you are consistently in about the same place on the scale, consider whether greater flexibility of approach might help make you a more effective leader.

Factors in your team

So much for the leader. What about the led? The extent to which you can appropriately share decision-making with them depends on the factors listed below. Thinking of your staff, which of the seven approaches (**a–g**) would be most appropriate with them?

- Their beliefs about who should be making the
  decisions and saying what is to be done   **a b c d e f g**

- Their experience of taking responsibility for
  decision-making   **a b c d e f g**

- Their willingness to take responsibility (and risk
  making decisions for which they'll no longer be able
  to blame you)   **a b c d e f g**

- The degree to which they feel that the problems or
  decisions are important enough to be worth spending
  their time and energy on   **a b c d e f g**

If your staff think you are the one paid to make the decisions, have no experience in making them, are generally unwilling to risk having no one to blame but themselves and/or think the problems are trivial or routine – then you would ideally need to be more directive than if they thought otherwise.

Factors in the task

The appropriate style of leadership depends not only on factors in the leader and the led, but also on factors in the task or project about which decisions have to be made. Consider how the following factors might suggest approaches towards one end of the scale (**a–g**) rather than the other.

- A routine standardized task   a b c d e f g
- An open-ended innovative task   a b c d e f g
- A difficult and complex problem   a b c d e f g
- A straightforward problem   a b c d e f g
- The task is to be completed fast   a b c d e f g
- The time scale can be stretched   a b c d e f g
- There is no room for error   a b c d e f g
- Errors can be corrected   a b c d e f g

The more routine and straightforward the task, and the less time you have for it and the less room for error, the more a directive approach may be called for. But you may be able to change the nature of the task more easily than you can change any of the other three variables if you want to adopt whatever style it is that they suggest.

Factors in the organization

Even if you can adjust your style of leadership to suit your team and the task, you may still be limited by what is acceptable within your organization, or within your part of it. Consider which leadership styles each of the following factors might push you towards.

- A bureaucratic organization where there are rules and procedures covering all tasks   a b c d e f g
- An organization that depends on individual initiatives and independent projects   a b c d e f g
- The emphasis within the organization is on creativity and grasping opportunities   a b c d e f g
- The emphasis is on avoiding mistakes and the punishments that always result from them   a b c d e f g
- Each unit within the organization must run on the same lines as every other and/or its work must interlock with that of others   a b c d e f g

- Different units are free to develop their own best
  ways of working   a b c d e f g

- Your manager encourages the managers he or she is
  responsible for to use whatever leadership styles
  they find most effective   a b c d e f g

- Your manager says 'Managers are here to manage'   a b c d e f g

Remember, different factors in the organization, the task and the people in your team will favour different approaches to leadership. Your success as a leader is likely to depend on how flexible you can be in adapting your own behaviour to provide what is appropriate in the different circumstances.

A leader's checklist

A leader is responsible both for getting tasks performed and for the people performing them. The following checklist, which you may find worth consulting every few weeks, should help you keep this in mind.

Which of the following activities have you carried out in the last month?

- Shared with my staff my enthusiasm about what they are
  doing and reminded them how it fits in with the work of
  the organization as a whole   ❏

- Arranged for my team's work to be allocated among
  individuals in such a way as to promote the satisfactory
  development of those individuals as well as the
  accomplishment of the task   ❏

- Told or reminded each individual about the purpose and
  importance of his or her work   ❏

- Given each individual constructive comments on his or
  her work   ❏

- Helped individuals to improve at their jobs (and become
  capable of more challenging tasks)   ❏

- Reviewed people's jobs with a view to making them more
  satisfying   ❏

- Taken each individual's views into account in agreeing/ revising his or her targets or objectives ❑
- Involved individuals in decision-making where appropriate ❑
- Delegated decision-making where appropriate ❑
- Explained all decisions I have taken myself ❑
- Been responsive to suggestions and grievances ❑
- Ensured that individuals who have broken important rules have not been allowed to get away with it ❑
- Encouraged staff to join a union (if one is recognized) and to take an active part ❑
- Monitored our operation and kept my team informed – in such a way that we all learn from experience (of our failures as well as our successes) ❑
- Made sure that all members of my team know of events or decisions elsewhere in the organization (or outside) that may affect our operation ❑
- Defended my staff if their work has been criticized by someone outside the team ❑
- Shown my staff that I care about them as individuals and recognized that their work will be affected by what is happening in the rest of their lives (and vice versa) – as will mine ❑

N.B. Many managers think they do all these things as a matter of course, yet their staff think otherwise.

KEY IDEA

Leadership consists of getting an operation done by other people. Don't concentrate on the operation and neglect the people, or concentrate on the people to the neglect of the operation.

CHAPTER THREE

Managing finance

Contents

Introduction

As managers, we can't avoid thinking about money. Whatever kind of operation we're running, the finances cannot be ignored. At the very least, we're probably trying to make sure our operation doesn't cost more than it needs to. Perhaps we're also expecting our operation to make money, even to show a profit.

So there are many financial aspects to the issues we discuss in **Managing operations**, (page 51) – especially in **Planning**, (page 60) and **Controlling** (page 71).

In planning a project or operation, we realize that we can only achieve our objectives through the use of resources. And resources mean money. So we need a budget that sets out what money we need, and when. Sometimes we may be negotiating for a slice of someone else's budget. At other times we may be arguing the case for having a budget of our own for a particular project or activity.

Then, while the project or operation is under way, we need to control it. Among the factors we'll need to monitor is how the money is flowing (in and out). We'll need to monitor income and costs. And take appropriate action if our finances are not working out as we budgeted.

Thoughtful financial management should help you avoid reliving the despair of the overstretched Robinson Crusoe:

'Now I saw, though too late, the Folly of beginning a Work before we count the Cost, and before we judge rightly of our Strength to go through with it'!

Preparing a budget

In planning a project or activity, you will need to think about likely income and expenditure. (See the checklists on **Planning**, page 60.) That is, you will need to prepare a budget – and one that will persuade whoever holds the purse strings in your organization to let you have the resources you need. Here are some questions to bear in mind.

- What are the goals (targets, objectives or expected outcomes) of the project or activity you are budgeting for?

- Have you considered all realistic ways of achieving these goals (and their costs and benefits) before choosing the most appropriate?

- Are you clear what benefits the project or activity will provide – e.g. in terms of the objectives of your section and the organization as a whole?

- How best can you estimate the likely costs and possible income arising from various aspects of the project or activity?

- Might it be useful to consult members of your team or other colleagues who have appropriate experience?

- What can you learn from reviewing your budgets for previous similar projects or activities (if any) that might help you in refining this one?

- Are the outcomes of previous budgets worth mentioning in support of the budget you are proposing now? For example, might they help justify what you want to spend or the levels of income you predict?

- If you haven't previously prepared a budget, might one of your fellow managers or another colleague be able to show you some of their successful budgets and/or offer useful tips?

- Are you clear on the assumptions you have made about the situation you are budgeting for, why you have made them and how realistic they are?

- Have you done your best to take account of every contingency that might possibly arise and upset your income or expenditure?

- Do you need to check out your budget (and its underlying assumptions) with members of your team or with specialist colleagues (e.g. accountants) before presenting it for approval?

KEY IDEA

Members of your team may be more likely to try to achieve the benefits aimed for in your budget if you involve them in its preparation.

Negotiating and agreeing a budget

Having prepared a budget, you now need to get other people's agreement. This will no doubt involve you in meetings and negotiations. (And you may need to revise the budget before you finally get agreement.) See the checklists on **Negotiating** (page 38).

Preparing for the negotiations

- To whom must you present your proposed budget?
- What 'house rules' (e.g. special forms and jargon), if any, must you follow in presenting it?
- If you need to present it to more than one person or group (e.g. your manager, your manager's manager, a committee) do you need to do so differently in each case?
- Have you anticipated all the doubts or objections people may want to raise about your budget – and prepared extra information or arguments to satisfy or counter them?
- If you won't be presenting your proposed budget in person, how will you ensure that the extra material is available if needed (e.g. by preparing an optional appendix or by briefing a colleague who will be involved in discussing your proposal)?
- Can you make quite clear what benefits the expenditure will provide – e.g. in terms of the objectives of your section and the organization as a whole?
- Can you also be quite clear in your own mind about what the effects would be on your operation if you were to get less than what you are asking for?

When you are ready

- Present your budget as early as possible, so as to leave you time to do further work on it should this be required of you.

- If you get the chance to introduce your budget documents orally before discussion begins, ensure that you concentrate on the key issues and avoid too much detail.

- Emphasize the benefits that your proposed expenditure will provide – e.g. in terms of the objectives of your section and the organization as a whole.

- If appropriate, emphasize also (rather more delicately, perhaps) any benefits to the individuals with whom you are negotiating.

- Take a 'win–win' approach in your negotiations (see the checklists on **Negotiating**, page 38).

- If people express doubts or objections, try to treat them as constructive critics and enlist their help in strengthening your budget.

- Be ready to reply with your 'extra information' (see the fourth point under **Preparing for the negotiations** opposite) where you judge this would be helpful.

- If you are forced to cut back on certain aspects of your budget, consider whether there are any alternative resources you might ask for as 'compensation'.

- Make sure that everyone concerned appreciates what results can *not* be expected from your operation, given a reduced budget.

- If you are asked to do further work on your budget, try to get the people who asked to spell out exactly what would satisfy them.

- Discuss the outcome of the budget negotiations with your team as soon as possible, so they know what you are wanting them to commit themselves to.

KEY IDEA

Don't waste time in regrets if you don't get all you asked for. Concentrate instead on doing the best possible job with whatever resources you do get.

Monitoring your budget

So, you now have an agreed budget. Maybe you've been given exactly the resources you asked for, maybe less (and maybe, just possibly, more). You now have the responsibility of keeping to that budget. This means that you must monitor your operation's spending (and income, if any) and look out for 'variances' from budget.

- Ensure that you have a system for collecting and recording accurate information about income and expenditure.
- Check this information regularly, at appropriate intervals.
- If your *income* is bigger or smaller than expected during some period, what effect is this likely to have in later periods or overall?
- Do you need to take any action to make up for or build on this income variance?
- If your *expenditure* is bigger or smaller than expected during some period, what effect is this likely to have in later periods or overall?
- Do you need to take any action to make up for or build on this expenditure variance?
- If you need to take corrective action, do so promptly.
- Ensure that you do not spoil your cash flow by overspending in one period of your budget, even though you will still be within your budget over the year.
- Ensure that all relevant team members know how the budget is working out and are kept informed of any corrective action that needs to be taken and what result it has had.
- If you realize that you may need to spend more resources in one area of your budget (and less in another), seek agreement from the relevant people as soon as possible.
- If you look like spending more (or less) than your overall budget, let the relevant people know as soon as possible.
- Reflect on what you have learned from the experience of monitoring this budget that might lead you to do things differently next time you monitor a budget (or prepare or negotiate one).

KEY IDEA

Don't be so determined to keep precisely to your budget that you inhibit yourself from responding appropriately to new opportunities that present themselves.

Controlling your costs

It may not be one of the purposes of your operation to generate income. But even though you may not be generating income, you will be generating costs. And, whatever your purposes, you'll be expected to achieve them with as little outlay of resources as possible. That is, you will be expected to keep your costs to what you have budgeted – and reduce them still further where you see ways of doing so.

Preparing to control your costs

- Make sure you know what kinds of costs you are responsible for, under headings such as these:
    - labour costs
    - materials costs
    - overhead costs
    - fixed costs
    - variable costs
    - production costs
    - administrative costs
    - marketing costs
    - selling costs
    - costs determined by outside forces.
- Work out what you have budgeted to spend under all appropriate cost headings.
- Check that your system enables you to collect information rapidly about expenditure under all appropriate headings.
- Seek to set up an early warning system to alert you if some costs are likely to rise in the future (e.g. costs from an outside supplier).
- Make sure that each member of your team knows the area of costs that they have an influence on.
- Ask for their suggestions as to how costs in their areas might be reduced (without weakening the operation).
- Get their commitment to specific reductions in cost where appropriate (if necessary by offering something they want).

- Decide how frequently you will review the records on costs incurred so far.

Exercising control

- Review the records on costs at the intervals you decided, and more often if necessary.
- Where costs have risen beyond budget, find out why.
- Take prompt action, where possible, to correct whatever factors have caused costs to be unexpectedly high.
- Where possible, do what is necessary to ensure that these factors do not cause costs to get too high again in future.
- Where you cannot do anything to eliminate these factors, decide what you can do to make up for the overspend.
- Where costs have risen to the point where you know you will exceed your budget, report this to the appropriate people as soon as possible.
- If they can suggest corrective action that you have not already taken, take it.
- If you are incurring costs on behalf of another section, let them know promptly if those costs are likely to be higher than expected (e.g. because of outside forces).
- Keep members of your team informed about how the operation is doing in terms of keeping costs under control.
- To save cost control from getting a totally negative image, remember to praise and encourage those staff who have contributed to keeping costs down.
- What have you learned from this experience of controlling costs that might lead you to do things differently in future?

KEY IDEA

Make friends with your accountants. Sometimes only they can help you save your operation from crisis.

CHAPTER FOUR

Managing people

Contents

Introduction

Much of your success as a manager will depend on the quality of the people whose work you are responsible for. You may think this is not entirely under your control. It is true that most of us inherit a ready-made team when we first take on a managerial role. But sooner or later vacancies arise and we get the chance to appoint people of our own choosing. No matter how you come by your staff, you can expect to influence the morale and productivity of your team by the way you set about understanding their strengths and weaknesses, developing their competences, improving people's jobs, coaching and counselling them, appraising their work, encouraging their efforts, ensuring equal opportunities and where necessary applying disciplinary procedures. In short, while your success is dependent on your team's results, those results will depend on your leadership and performance management skills. So the checklists in this section are about choosing new people for your team and fostering the morale and productivity of everyone in it.

Knowing your team

Who have you got working with you? What are their strengths and weaknesses, their interests and dislikes, and which of them get on together and which detest one another? In short, how well do you *know* your team? The better you know them, the more likely you are to get them to work to the best of their ability.

If you were once a member of the team yourself, you should know them pretty well. If you chose all the members yourself, then you presumably know quite a lot about them as individuals – though you may not yet know how well they will work together as a team. But most managers get a ready-made team wished upon them. If you are in this position you will need to be systematic in getting to know and understand your team members – both as individuals and as *interacting* members of a working group.

The following checklists should help you in this.

Basic facts

- How many staff are you directly responsible for?

  _____

- How old is each member of staff?

  _____

- How many of each sex?

  _____

- How long has each been:
  - in the organization?   _____

    _____

  - in this section?   _____

    _____

- Which have had experience (and how much) of related work in other organizations/sections?

Who does what?

	Yes	No
Does each member of your team have a job description?	❏	❏
If not, should you work with them to develop one?	❏	❏
Even without a formal job description, are each member of staff's duties and/or work targets clear to them (and to you)?	❏	❏
Do any members of your team feel that too much or too little is being demanded of them?	❏	❏
Are any members of your team deficient in the skills or knowledge they need for the work they are currently doing?	❏	❏
Are any individuals performing less than acceptably at present?	❏	❏

	Yes	No

- Could any members of your team benefit from a change of duties? ❏ ❏
- Could any of your team benefit from further training to:
  - improve their present work? ❏ ❏
  - prepare them for new duties? ❏ ❏

See the checklists on **Coaching and training** (page 133) **Improving people's jobs** (page 142) and **Motivating your team** (page 146).

Relationships

	Yes	No

- Is it important for the members of your team to collaborate with one another? ❏ ❏
- Is the general atmosphere within the team one of:
  - mutual support and co-operation? ❏ ❏
  - competition and selfishness? ❏ ❏
- Do some members of your team work as loners, effectively but without regularly collaborating with other members? ❏ ❏
- Are there other loners who do not work effectively and who need to be helped to work collaboratively with others? ❏ ❏
- Are there members of the team who ought to be encouraged to work more independently of the others? ❏ ❏
- Do any of the team members seem markedly less accepted by the group than others do? ❏ ❏
- If so, why? And what effect does it have on the morale and productivity of the team? _____

  _____

- Does the group have any members on whom it habitually blames its shortcomings (scapegoats) or on whom it vents its frustrations and hostilities (whipping boys/girls)? ❏ ❏

	Yes	No

- Are there any obvious moaners, stirrers or troublemakers who will delight in giving you (and other members of the team) a bad time? ❏ ❏

- Who are the *opinion leaders* in your team – those to whom the others are likely to look for informal leadership (especially in your absence)? _____

  _____

- What sort of image did the manager who preceded you (if any) have with the team? _____

  _____

- What are the team expecting from you? _____

  _____

Personalities

Don't be tempted to write down your answers to the following questions – a leak could be embarrassing.

- In a couple of words, how would you describe the personality of each member of your team?

- Which team members do you feel you could most rely on in a crisis or when effort beyond the normal call of duty is called for?

- Which team members seem least to be relied upon?

- To whom would you look as a source of bright ideas or as someone on whom to sound out promising ideas of your own?

- Which team members would be most/least resistant to changing their ways of working?

- Which of your team members is first to know what is going on within the group and how people are feeling about things?

- Thinking about each member of your team in turn, does he or she seem to owe first loyalty to:
  - the organization?

- the section?
- their trade or profession, be it catering or accountancy?

- Think again about each member of your team in turn. Which of the following do you feel each would regard as a major source of satisfaction in his or her work:
  - good wages or salary?
  - the prospect of promotion?
  - official fringe benefits (perks)?
  - unofficial fringe benefits?
  - getting as much free time as possible?
  - the satisfaction of turning out high-quality work?
  - getting good feedback from customers/clients?
  - the prospect of developing new expertise?
  - the easy life of undemanding routine work?
  - the challenge of changing, variable work?
  - contributing to a worthwhile enterprise/
  - gaining personal status or power?
  - agreeable working conditions?
  - being told exactly what to do?
  - having some freedom to decide how they work?
  - the feeling of being needed?
  - social relationships with workmates?
  - being respected within the organization?
  - being respected by outsiders?
  - others _____

- While you're at it you may as well ask the same question of yourself – which of the factors mentioned in the list above do *you* feel most motivated by?

The reputation of your team

	Yes	No
• Is your team respected by other sections of the organization?	❏	❏
• Does it have any rivals or enemies?	❏	❏

	Yes	No
• Is the style of dress, speech, discipline, working methods, etc. broadly similar to that in other teams?	❏	❏
• Does your team have *official* working relationships with other teams?	❏	❏
• Do individuals have close *informal* relationships with individuals in other teams?	❏	❏
• Can they obtain advance warning about how your team is seen by others?	❏	❏
• Was the manager who preceded you (if any) regarded favourably by the majority of influential people in the organization?	❏	❏
• Which individuals in the organization have most influence on how your team is regarded by the rest of the organization? _____		

Needless to say you will not gather the kind of information outlined above by sending around a questionnaire. Nor can you expect to gather it overnight. Learning about your staff will be a never-ending occupation – not least because they will be changing all the time you know them (in part because of your influence on them and the experiences you go through together). Mainly you will learn by talking with them, by noticing how they respond to everyday situations, and by listening to what people outside your team have to say about them. The more you learn about them, the better you will work together.

KEY IDEA

If you really want to know your staff, pay more attention to what they do than to what they say – but don't ignore what other people say about them.

Planning for new staff

As a manager you will have some responsibility for appointing new staff. This has three aspects.

1. Deciding what jobs you need new staff for.

2. Deciding what sort of people you need to fill those jobs.

3. Finding such people.

The following set of checklists will help you with the first two tasks and the next set (**Selection interviewing**, page 126) will help you with the third. You may or may not have some sort of help from personnel specialists. Even if you do, remember that you, not they, are the one who has to take responsibility for the *work* of the people appointed.

Analyzing the job

Here are the questions to ask yourself long before you reach for your pen and start drafting a job advertisement.

	Yes	No
● Why does there appear to be a vacancy?:		
– has someone left?	❏	❏
– are there new tasks to be done?	❏	❏
– has the volume of work increased?	❏	❏
● Do we really need an extra person?:		
– can we get along without the person who's leaving?	❏	❏
– can we retrain existing staff to perform new tasks?	❏	❏
– can we increase our productivity, using new methods or equipment?	❏	❏
● If we really do need someone, has the job already been analyzed for payment or training purposes?	❏	❏
● If so, does that analysis still describe how I would like the new person to work?	❏	❏
● If the vacancy arises because someone is leaving, do I want someone who will do exactly the same work as that person?	❏	❏
● How do I decide exactly what work needs doing?:		
– by discussion with people currently doing the work (in my section or elsewhere)?	❏	❏

	Yes	No
– by observing them doing the work?	❏	❏
– by discussion with other managers?	❏	❏
– by considering how to achieve important objectives that are not being achieved at present?	❏	❏

- What will the job involve?:
  - why will it be done? (what is its purpose?) _____

    _____

  - what will be done? _____

    _____

  - what will result from it? _____

    _____

  - when will it be done? _____

    _____

  - where will it be done? _____

    _____

  - how will it be done? _____

    _____

  - what standards of performance will be required? _____

    _____

- What responsibility will the job-holder have for:
  - team members? _____

    _____

  - money? _____

    _____

  - equipment or materials? _____

    _____

  - confidential information? _____

    _____

  - deciding his or her own work methods? _____

    _____

  - deciding his or her own objectives or targets? _____

    _____

- What working relationships (formal or informal) will the job-holder have?:

- with me? _____

- with other team members? _____

- with other managers? _____

- with members of other teams? _____

- with outsiders (e.g. customers or suppliers)? _____

● What will be the job's:
  - pay and economic rewards? _____

  - physical working conditions? _____

  - social conditions? _____

  - most challenging or attractive features? _____

  - most difficult or distasteful features? _____

● Do I need to check my answers to the last four questions by discussion with:

	Yes	No
- job-holders?	❏	❏
- my manager?	❏	❏
- other managers?	❏	❏
- personnel specialists?	❏	❏

● Can I now write a satisfactory job description based on these answers, and using headings such as the following?

	Yes	No
- Job title	❏	❏
- Main purpose of job	❏	❏
- Chief duties and activities	❏	❏
- Specific responsibilities	❏	❏
- Working relationships	❏	❏

	Yes	No
– Pay and conditions	❑	❑
– Others _____		

Describing the person for the job

Once you've analyzed what needs doing and described the job, you are ready to describe the sort of person who will be needed to do it. This description is sometimes called a *personnel specification*. Here are the chief aspects to consider.

Education

● What level of general education does the work require?

● What qualifications (if any) are necessary?

Training

● Is any kind of specific job-related training required?

● If so, can it be provided after a person is appointed?

Experience

● What type and length of previous experience is needed?

General intelligence

● What level of general mental ability is required?

● Are some kinds of mental ability more essential than others – e.g. verbal versus spatial versus numerical?

Specific abilities

● What specific competences and knowledge does the work call for?

● Must the new person have acquired all of these *before* beginning the job?

● What evidence of these abilities shall we expect?

Personality

- What type of person will fit in best with the existing team?
- What social skills will the person need in all relevant working relationships?
- What kinds of disposition are required by the job – independence, docility, cheerfulness, accuracy, creativity, etc?

Physique and health

- Are there any requirements of height, weight or strength?
- Are hearing, eyesight or other aspects of health important?
- Are general appearance, dress sense or voice of relevance?

Personal circumstances

- How close to work would the job-holder need to live?
- Would the job-holder need to work irregular hours?
- Would he or she need to be free to travel?

N.B. With each of the above, be sure to think about what would be the *essential minimum* as well as the *desirable ideal*.

Does such a person exist?

Now you know what the vacancy is, and the kind of person you need to fill it, how confident can you be about finding them?

	Yes	No
● Do people with such a combination of desirable qualities exist anywhere?	❏	❏
● If so, will they be available in this area?	❏	❏
● And at this time of year?	❏	❏
● Why should he or she want the job? _____		

- Why should he or she want to join this particular
  organization? _____

  _____

- What would such people be earning now? _____

  _____

	Yes	No

- Can we offer enough in pay and/or other benefits to
  make a move seem worthwhile? ❏ ❏

- What will be my contingency plan in case an acceptable individual fails
  to appear? _____

  _____

Getting suitable applicants

The first step towards finding suitable applicants (assuming some exist) is
to bring the job to their attention.

- Before you think of advertising in a newspaper or journal,
  consider these (for the most part) cheaper alternatives.
  Tick any you think you might be able to use.
  - Invite an existing member of your team to take the
    post ❏
  - Ask team members to recommend friends or family ❏
  - Advertise *within* your organization (this may be
    required of you anyway) ❏
  - Consult the organization's files of unsuccessful
    applicants for similar previous posts ❏
  - Mention the job to any individuals you know in other
    organizations who might be suitable ❏
  - Ask friends in other organizations to mention the job
    to people who might be qualified and interested ❏
  - Contact your local government-operated employment
    service ❏

- Contact the appointments advisors of colleges and
  universities ❑
- Contact the commercial employment agencies and
  executive selection agencies ❑

● If you need to advertise externally, consider these factors:
  - What kind of advertising will bring me the applicants
    I want at the least possible cost?
  - How much can I afford to pay for advertising?
  - How much is it worth paying, considering the level
    of the job?
  - Where shall I advertise – local papers, nationals, trade
    or specialist journals, the Internet?
  - Have I seen other organizations' advertisements for
    similar vacancies – and do they have any features we
    should either follow or avoid?
  - What do we need to say in the advertisement, in order
    to attract suitable applicants – and discourage
    unsuitable ones?
  - Does our advertisement give sufficient detail about:
    - the name and nature of the organization? ❑
    - the job title? ❑
    - the nature of the job and its responsibilities? ❑
    - how the job relates to other jobs in the
      organization? ❑
    - where the job would be located? ❑
    - education and/or qualifications required? ❑
    - experience and/or training required? ❑
    - specific abilities required? ❑
    - personality features expected? ❑
    - age range? (if a restricted range can be justified) ❑
    - requirements of physique or health? ❑
    - pay and other benefits? ❑
    - working conditions? ❑
    - how and by when the application should be made? ❑
  - Who drafts the advertisement and who must approve it?
  - Apart from attracting (we hope) the right kind of

applicants, does the advertisement present the
appropriate public image of our organization?

- Does it, above all, avoid any suggestion that preference
  will be given to people of one sex or age or ethnic
  origin or religious belief rather than another?

- However you intend to obtain applicants, do you want
  them to:
  - complete an application form? ❏
  - just tell you whatever they think is relevant in a letter
    of application? or ❏
  - send both a form and a letter? ❏

- If your organization does not have a standard application form, you
  may want to devise one of your own, covering the key points about
  which you'll need information in order to draw up a shortlist.

- Will you be sending further particulars to people who enquire about
  the job? (This could include, or be based on, the job description and
  personnel specification – but it might also give details about the work
  of the organization and about the selection procedure you'll be using.)

Dealing with applications

Here are the questions you'll need to ask yourself before the applications
start flooding in.

- What sort of clerical system do I need to set up in order to:
  - handle telephone calls and e-mails?
  - send out application forms and further particulars when they are
    asked for?
  - record the names and addresses of people they are sent to?
  - record and acknowledge the return of completed applications?
  - agree a suitable date and time with applicants who are to be
    interviewed?
  - send a courteous letter to unsuccessful applicants?
  - contact applicants' referees?
  - carry out any other tasks _____

- How much personal attention must I give to this system in order to ensure that it:
  - runs smoothly?
  - does nothing to harm the image of the organization in the eyes of applicants?
- From perhaps dozens of applicants, how do I draw up a shortlist of, say, half a dozen candidates for interviewing?
  - Be systematic about it – don't go by 'general impressions'.
  - Be prepared to read through the applications several times.
  - Compare each applicant with the personnel specification.
  - Eliminate any who do not meet *essential* requirements.
  - If you still have too many applicants, eliminate those who do not meet *desirable* requirements.
  - Of those that are left, choose those who seem closest to your ideal applicant.
  - In addition to those you shortlist, pick out a couple of reserve applicants in case some of those you invite for interview decide to withdraw their applications.
  - If possible, get like-minded colleagues to draw up shortlists, using criteria similar to yours, and discuss any differences between you.

KEY IDEA

Be prepared to readvertise (or else lower your requirements) if suitable applicants have not been forthcoming.

Selection interviewing

Having drawn up your shortlist of candidates (see the checklists on **Planning for new staff**, page 117), you will want to interview them. The interview has been described as a conversation with a purpose. Actually, it has at least three purposes.

1. To enable *you* to discover which of the candidates live up to expectations and which one of them best meets the job's requirements.
2. To enable *them* to find out about the job and the organization and to decide whether they really want to work with you.

3. To leave them (whether successful or rejected) with a favourable impression of the organization and feeling none the worse about themselves as a result of the interview.

Most managers think they are good at interviewing. But it is not easy to do well. Researchers have shown, over and over again, that interviewers fail in their task because they make up their minds too early, fail to collect all the relevant information or don't evaluate systematically what has emerged from the interview.

Furthermore, interviewers rarely get evidence that any of their rejected candidates would have been a better choice. So – unless the person they do appoint turns out to be obviously incompetent – they are rarely prompted even to reflect on their mistakes.

Nevertheless, interviews continue to be the most common method of selecting new staff. So it is worth thinking about how to avoid the major pitfalls. The following checklists cover:

- preparing for the interview;
- conducting the interview;
- evaluating the interview.

Preparing for the interview

Here are the questions to ask yourself by way of preparation.

- How many candidates shall I be interviewing?
- Have I allowed plenty of time for each candidate?
- Shall I be the only interviewer?
- Will candidates need to meet other members of staff besides the interviewer(s)?
- When might such meetings best take place?
- Who will welcome the candidates and look after them on the day of the interviews?

- Will there be a convenient room available – with comfortable seating, a glass of water for the candidate, an ashtray (if I don't mind the candidate smoking), and so on?

- Do I need candidates to bring certificates or proof of qualifications?

- Do I need candidates to bring samples of their previous work, or even to prepare a sample specially?

- In addition to the interview, shall I be expecting candidates to do any kind of test or exercise that simulates the sort of work required by the job?

- Who will write a friendly letter to the shortlisted candidates:
  - thanking them for applying
  - inviting them to come for interview
  - telling them when and where it will take place
  - offering to consider an alternative time if necessary
  - telling them who will be interviewing them
  - mentioning any certificates or other items they need to bring with them
  - letting them know if there will be any formal tests as well as the interview
  - asking for any important information that was missing from their applications
  - giving them any other relevant information (e.g. maps, expenses claim forms, etc.)?

- What documents/information will I need to take with me to the interview? For example:
  - job description?
  - personnel specification?
  - further particulars?
  - candidates' applications?
  - referees' reports?
  - any other details about the job or the organization that might be needed to answer candidates' questions?

- How shall I structure the interview? For example:
  - What areas of questioning do I wish to cover?

- If I am interviewing with colleagues, how are we to divide the areas of questioning between us?
- Shall I begin by talking about the job for which the candidate has applied?
- At what point do I start taking the candidate through important points in his/her application?
- Do I need to ask for a demonstration or evidence of the candidate's skills?
- How shall I find out about how the candidate sees his/her career progression so far?
- How can I enable the candidate to discover all he/she can about whether the job is likely to further his/her career plans?
- Approximately how much time shall I allow for each of these areas of discussion?

N.B. Make sure you cover the same ground with every candidate or comparisons will be impossible.

Conducting the interview

Sequence

Is this a suitable sequence for your interviews to follow?

1 Put the candidate at his/her ease – e.g. by going to the waiting room, introducing yourself in a relaxed and friendly way, making sociable conversation while accompanying them to the interview room.

2 Introduce the other interviewers (if any). (Should each interviewer have a name card in front of them?)

3 Briefly mention some of the main points about the job and your organization. (This may highlight what the candidate has already seen in the further particulars.)

4 Draw out the candidate's career biography by:
   - spending most time on his/her most recent work;
   - getting the candidate to talk about his/her successes (without avoiding less successful aspects);

- discussing relations with colleagues (and managers);
- determining what has moved the candidate to change jobs;
- asking what the candidate expects from this new job.

5 Examine samples of the candidate's work, or a practical demonstration of his/her abilities, if appropriate.

6 At the end of the interview, invite the candidate to:

- mention or expand on any of his/her experience or expertise that has not been adequately covered;

- ask *you* any questions that have not already been answered.

7 Tell the candidate what to expect now the interview is over – how, and by when, candidates will know whether they are to be made an offer.

Questioning techniques

Your success in getting useful information from the candidate will depend on your ability to ask appropriate kinds of questions. The most basic distinction is between *closed* questions (which invite a 'yes', 'no' or other very brief response) and *open* questions (which invite a more expansive and thoughtful answer).

- Use *open* questions when you want to:
  - introduce new areas of discussion (e.g. *What attracted you to your present job?*)
  - explore further (*Could you tell me more about that?*)
  - link one response with an earlier one (*How did that affect the conflicts you mentioned earlier?*)
  - probe self-awareness (*In what ways did the course change your attitudes?*)
  - get candidates to demonstrate their approach to problem-solving (*How might you tackle that problem now?*).

- Use *closed* questions only when:
  - 'yes' or a 'no' is all you require (*Are you a member?*)
  - some other very specific response will suffice (*Just over 2 years*)
  - you intend to follow up with an open question (*So why did you leave?*).

- Use open questions much more frequently than closed ones (or you'll find yourself doing most of the talking, and probably sounding like an interrogator).
- Avoid:
  - leading questions – those that tell the candidate what kind of answer you expect (*Wouldn't you agree that . . .?*)
  - package questions (*What is your main task at the moment, and how does it compare with what you were doing before and what do you want to go on to next?*)
  - unfair questions – especially about the job you are interviewing for which the candidate could not possibly be expected to answer without far more detailed knowledge than he/she can possibly possess at present
  - trick questions of any kind that serve no purpose but to suggest that the interviewer is smarter than the candidate
  - giveaway questions that suggest to the candidates (or to your fellow interviewers) that you have already decided for or against them
  - questions that offend against equal opportunities legislation or your organization's policy, (e.g. asking a young married man or woman: *What arrangements do you have for looking after your children?*)

Controlling the interview

An interview is neither a one-way interrogation nor a free-and-easy conversation. It is a *structured* conversation in which one of the participants (the candidate) should be doing most of the talking – at least two-thirds of it. Your ability to keep the discussion flowing to best effect will depend on:

- The sort of questions you ask and the order in which you ask them (see **Questioning techniques**, opposite).
- The close *attention* you pay to the candidate's replies, silences and body language.
- The degree to which you can guard against making up your mind about the candidate too early and noticing only those things that support that premature judgement.

- How well you listen to and take into account the questions asked and the replies received by the *other* interviewers (if any). (See the checklists on **Listening**, page 209.)

- How *you* use your own body language and non-verbal communication:
  - nodding or smiling;
  - looking at the candidate or at notes, other interviewers, etc.;
  - leaning towards the candidate or away;
  - standing up or walking about;
  - tolerating silences;
  - grunts (like *uh-huh* or *Mmmm*);
  - closing the file and putting your pen in your pocket.

Evaluating the interview

There are two aspects to this:

1. evaluating each candidate (preferably before seeing the next as well as after seeing all candidates);
2. evaluating the conduct and outcome of the interview.

Evaluating each candidate

- Does the candidate have the *ability* to do the job well?
- Does he/she have enough *motivation* to do it well?
- Would he/she *fit in* with the rest of the team?
- Is any candidate satisfactory on all three of these criteria?
- If not, do you lower your standards or readvertise?
- If more than one candidate meets all three criteria, which one do you prefer, and why?

Evaluating the interviewing

- Do you feel reasonably confident about the chosen candidate?
- Did you get the kind of information you needed out of the interview?
- Which aspects of the interview were least satisfactory?

- Could you have improved them by better planning, questioning, listening, etc?
- Can you see any ways to improve the selection process next time?
- Check on the performance of the selected candidate over the next few months. How does it compare with what you expected? (Unfortunately, you will never know whether people you rejected might have done even better!)
- Does this comparison suggest any necessary changes in the selection process?

KEY IDEA

Keep an open mind throughout the interview. If you feel particularly for or against a candidate, look especially for information that might contradict that feeling.

Coaching and training

As a manager, your most precious resource is your staff – the people whose work you are responsible for. Without them you are superfluous. Only through their efforts can you (and the organization) achieve anything worthwhile. The greater the ability and willingness of your staff, the more fruitful are these efforts likely to be.

Naturally, when you select new staff you will hope to select the most willing and able. But your responsibility does not end there. Sometimes you will select new staff or promote existing staff in the belief that they are willing and able to *learn* the new job. Now you have to arrange things so that they can do so. Even the best of recruits is likely to need your help in developing new abilities and understandings. At the very least, they need to learn how their present abilities can be adapted to serve and support the goals of the team they are joining. New staff cannot be expected to become effective in their new jobs without undertaking new learning.

More than this, however, even established staff will sooner or later find their abilities and understandings inadequate. They will need to learn new ways and improve on the old ones. Why so? Largely because of the rate at which things change nowadays. The goals of organizations change, as do the resources available to them. Similarly jobs change. New technologies entail new procedures, new roles and new relationships with others. Part of your managerial role is to be alert to the changing demands on your team and to consider how the individuals within it need to develop their skills and abilities and perhaps learn new ways of looking at things.

Even if your organization has a specialist training section you will have a continuing responsibility for identifying your own team's training *needs*. Whatever specialist training may be available, you will remain the person most capable of tackling many of those needs yourself – through one-to-one *coaching*.

Inducting new staff

Induction is your opportunity to help new staff to understand what's going on. This is essential even for staff who are merely transferring from another section in the organization. And there is more to it than just learning what work is required of them. The quicker you can help them tune in to the goals and expectations of your organization and your team – and how various people and sections relate to one another – the more quickly they will become effective team members.

	Yes	No
● Does your organization already have a formal induction programme for new staff?	❏	❏
● If so, do you know as much as you feel you should about what happens to new staff by way of induction?	❏	❏
● Is there an induction programme specially geared to the needs of people coming to work within your particular section or team?	❏	❏

● Is there anything extra you feel you or your team should be doing to inform your new staff about aspects of the

organization as a whole or about your team in particular?
Tick any aspects that might be worth additional attention:

	Org	Team
– history	❏	❏
– purposes or objectives	❏	❏
– customers' or clients' needs	❏	❏
– funding	❏	❏
– products or services	❏	❏
– competitors	❏	❏
– structure	❏	❏
– internal politics	❏	❏
– current problems or concerns	❏	❏
– emerging opportunities	❏	❏
– official rules and expectations	❏	❏
– unwritten rules and expectations	❏	❏
– staff rights and facilities	❏	❏

	Yes	No
● Is it appropriate to get new staff to visit other sections (near or distant) within the organization?	❏	❏
● Will there be opportunities for new staff to get a response to their *individual* queries/concerns?	❏	❏
● Will new staff be given some kind of *printed* reminder of the main points raised in the induction and an indication as to where to go for further information subsequently?	❏	❏

● How long will induction need to last? _____

_____

● Should it be done in one continuous splurge or be spread out over a period? _____

_____

● In addition to carrying out the induction training, how much time will be needed for planning it, for monitoring it and, when necessary, for modifying it? _____

_____

- If you already have, or wish to take, responsibility for some or all aspects of inducting your new staff, who will plan, organize and carry it out? _____

_____

Identifying training needs

There is often a gap between what people *can* do and what they *should* be able to do or would *like* to be able to do. This gap may indicate a training need. You may become aware of the training needs of individuals in your team through day-to-day contact with them. Or they may emerge in periodic reviews of their work (see the checklists on **Running a staff appraisal system**, page 163). Either way, questions like these may help you decide what is necessary.

1 What are my expectations about the way my team – and individuals and groups within it – should perform?

2 In what ways is an individual (or group) *not* performing as they should be?

3 How important is this gap in performance (e.g. cost, safety, output, etc.) compared with the amount of resources we might need to spend in closing it?

4 Does the gap in performance arise because the individual or group lacks the *ability* to perform as expected?

5 If they do lack the ability, did they once have it?

6 If they once had it, why have they lost it – can it be lack of practice and/or lack of feedback as to how they are performing?

7 If they have lost the ability, or never had it, would they be interested in acquiring it or reacquiring it?

8 Are they capable of acquiring it?

N.B. With **(7)** and **(8)**, avoid making assumptions about people's abilities or willingness to learn purely on the grounds of their race or ethnic origins, sex, marital status, age or whatever. Consider each one as an individual.

9 If they clearly *do* have the ability, why aren't they using it?
   – Do they know that they should use it (and when)?
   – Are there obstacles of time, equipment or interference that hinder them from performing as well as they could?
   – Are there penalties such as the danger of workmates' sneers for performing as they should?
   – Do individuals get greater (unofficial) rewards from performing 'their way' than from performing as well as they should?
   – Are they told immediately and clearly if their performance falls below what is expected of them?

10 Bearing in mind (3), would any of the following be cost-effective ways of closing the 'performance gap'?
   – Redeploying incapable/unwilling staff?
   – Selecting people who are more capable?
   – Redesigning jobs (e.g. simplify paperwork and procedures)?
   – Arranging more frequent practice of rarely performed tasks?
   – Providing job-aids (e.g. checklists or manuals) that remind people of how to perform such occasional tasks?
   – Taking more care in letting people know what they should be doing and when?
   – Encouraging groups to improve one another's abilities?
   – Providing on-the-job coaching?
   – Arranging for brief refresher training?
   – Arranging for full training courses?

N.B. Training (or coaching) may not be the solution to a performance problem (e.g. in the situations mentioned in **9**). Changes may be needed instead (or as well) in other areas such as selection, job design, supervision, communication and rewards.

11 You may be expected to identify your team's training needs, and/or to help individuals develop specific competences to meet the requirements of some *national* scheme (e.g. 'Investors in people' or NVQs and SVQs in the UK).
   – If so, do you know exactly what is expected of you by the scheme?
   – Do you know what is expected of you by your organization?

   – If you feel you need further briefing or training, who might provide it (e.g. your manager, the scheme's promoters, your personnel colleagues)?

Providing appropriate training

If you decided that certain people might benefit from training, how will you manage this? Certain forms of training (or staff development) are easier to arrange than others.

For instance, which of the following 'in-house' approaches might be acceptably effective in *your* circumstances?

- Throwing people in at the deep end? ❑
- Having them 'sit next to Nellie'? ❑
- Rotating them between jobs/tasks? ❑
- Seconding them to other sections? ❑
- Giving them special assignments? ❑
- Involving them in discussion groups? ❑
- Setting them guided reading? ❑
- Getting them to use self-teaching packages? ❑
- Having them practice under supervision? ❑
- Giving them regular direct instruction? ❑
- Coaching them informally? ❑
- Others _____

If you or one of your team ('Mr or Mrs Nellie') is going to give a member of staff direct instruction, there are some basic principles of teaching and learning that need observing.

- Put the learner at his or her ease.
- Explain the objectives of the instruction – i.e. what the learner might expect to be able to *do* (or do *better*) as a result of the instruction.

- Highlight the relevance of these objectives to the job.
- Check on the individual's present level of ability and understanding of what the job involves.
- Tell and/or show what has to be learned, step by step.
- Check the learner's understanding at each step – by getting them to *apply*, not just recall, what you have presented.
- Give feedback as to how well they have done this.
- Give them sufficient opportunity to practice each step before going on to the next.
- Praise what they do well and be patient and supportive when they are having difficulties.
- Be particularly alert for aspects in which the learner is repeatedly going wrong, and try to find out why – e.g. previous habits or misconceptions may be interfering with what they are trying to learn now.
- At frequent intervals, review what has been covered so far and check that the learner still has a grasp of it all.
- Don't overdo it by giving the learner more than they can absorb in a single session.
- When you come back to carry on the teaching, begin by checking that the learner can recall/do all they learned previously.
- Gradually be less and less ready to jump in with help – so that the learner increasingly has to make their own decisions.
- Keep an eye on the learner's work from day to day, offering further guidance where necessary.
- Be encouraging and non-threatening throughout – and try to avoid any kind of public criticism or correction that might lead to the learner losing face with co-workers.

Sometimes you will be able to provide adequate training (or coaching, which we deal with next) within your team. At other times you will need to look elsewhere within your organization, or even outside (locally or nationally), to find appropriate training for your staff. Tick any of the following you think might be worth considering for your staff.

- Sessions/courses within your organization ❏
- Local colleges or universities ❏
- Regional management centres ❏
- Business schools ❏
- Commercial training organizations ❏
- Government-funded schemes ❏
- Professional institutions ❏
- Trade unions ❏
- Employers' federations ❏
- Correspondence colleges ❏
- Open learning/distance teaching providers ❏

Coaching for success

Whether or not formal training or staff development is called for, you will still have a responsibility for *coaching*. This kind of training – giving continuous guidance and feedback to your staff in the light of what you see of their work – is often the most effective. It is also an unavoidable part of 'managing' (see the checklists on **Controlling**, page 71). Here are some pointers to bear in mind.

- Always remember your responsibility for helping to nurture and develop the abilities of each and every member of your team.
- Be alert to coaching opportunities wherever they arise – whether in an individual's work or a group's, or even through involving them in discussion of your problems or priorities.
- Choose your time for coaching. Sometimes it is necessary to pounce immediately if you see someone going badly wrong; at other times you will do better to let people reflect on their errors before they can benefit by discussing them.
- Never concentrate solely on errors. If you are going to criticize weaknesses, begin by making sure the individuals know how much you value their strengths.

- Don't try to tackle more than one or two weaknesses at a time.
- Give priority to those weaknesses that have most effect on the performance of the individual and the team.
- Encourage each individual's emerging strengths and look for ways to give people additional opportunities to exercise them.
- Make sure individuals know what you expect them to be doing and what you expect them to accomplish, preferably having discussed this with them first.
- But don't insist that everything be done your way (unless there is some supremely good reason why it must be). Ask people questions that get them thinking out *their own* better ways of doing things.
- Encourage people to consider alternative ways of doing things – and support them in their attempts to put new ways into practice.
- Identify other people in your team who could/should be coaching, and make it part of their duties to do so.
- Review your coaching week by week, and ensure that adequate time is being given to each individual.

N.B. Sometimes you may feel that an individual needs not so much 'coaching' as what you might be more inclined to think of as 'counselling' – for example where they have personal problems with other members of staff or anxieties about career stagnation or retirement. If so, look at the section on **Counselling your staff** (page 158) and consider whether you, or other colleagues in the organization, should offer to meet with them privately for a separate session.

KEY IDEA

Whatever you think you should or should not be doing about training, you will be training anyway. The example you set in your own working practices may well be the most powerful influence on how your staff choose to work.

Improving people's jobs

The more satisfaction people get from their work, the more likely they are to do it well and improve the productivity of their team. So can anything be done to modify a person's job so as to make it more satisfying?

You may or may not have much freedom to improve the jobs of the people in your team. The following checklists should help you decide what might be worth attempting where you can.

What is a satisfying job?

Below are some of the main features we might go for if we were trying to design a satisfying job for someone. Think about them in relation to each member of your team. Would each one agree that his or her job:

	Yes	No
– makes up some sort of *whole* – making an identifiable contribution to the team's and/or organization's eventual product or service?	❏	❏
– seems meaningful and worth doing?	❏	❏
– makes adequate calls on his or her skills and talents?	❏	❏
– provides sufficient variety in tasks or types of activity?	❏	❏
– allows him or her sufficient freedom to make decisions in doing the work?	❏	❏
– gives frequent enough feedback about the effectiveness of his or her performance?	❏	❏
– is reasonably demanding/challenging?	❏	❏
– provides adequate scope for learning and development?	❏	❏
– allows sufficient contact with colleagues?	❏	❏

N.B. Remember that individuals differ. What will seem 'adequate' or sufficient to one person may seem too much or too little to another. All the same, can you identify any of your team who might welcome your efforts to improve their jobs? Who? _____

Improving jobs

There are four standard approaches to improving jobs. These are:

1. job rotation;

2. job enlargement;

3. job enrichment;

4. autonomous working groups.

Consider these questions about each approach:

Job rotation

	Yes	No
● Could you arrange for any of your staff to rotate between different jobs in the team every few hours/days/weeks?	❑	❑
● Might there be any potential benefits for some individuals, e.g. a more satisfying variety of work?	❑	❑
● Would potential benefits be outweighed by negative factors, e.g. resentment at the break in routine?	❑	❑

Job enlargement

	Yes	No
● Could you arrange for any of your staff to carry out several similar tasks rather than just one of them – e.g. no longer carrying out just one of the four tasks in processing a customer's order, but carrying out all the tasks for one in every four orders?	❑	❑
● Might there be potential benefits for any individuals (e.g. more whole and meaningful work)?	❑	❑
● Would negative factors weigh more heavily – e.g. too much chopping and changing of tasks?	❑	❑

Job enrichment

	Yes	No

- Could you arrange for any of your staff to extend their jobs by, for example:
  - taking more responsibility for deciding their own objectives and/or way of working? ❏ ❏
  - using feedback to monitor their own performance? ❏ ❏
  - undertaking additional tasks that were previously regarded as higher level? ❏ ❏
  - acquiring and using new skills and expertise? ❏ ❏
- Might there be individuals who would benefit from the extra challenge and freedom to make their own decisions? ❏ ❏
- Or would they all prefer to settle for limited responsibility and not having to think too much about what they are doing? ❏ ❏

Autonomous working groups

	Yes	No

- Could you arrange to give your team, or *groups* within it, greater responsibility for planning, organizing and monitoring their work among themselves? ❏ ❏
- Might members of the group benefit from the closer working relationship with their colleagues? ❏ ❏
- Or might some people end up feeling less satisfied because of interpersonal problems? ❏ ❏

Possible advantages and disadvantages

Below is a list of possible advantages and a list of possible disadvantages of attempting to improve your people's jobs. Thinking about *your* situation, which of them might apply to job rotation (**R**), job enlargement (**L**), job enrichment (**E**) and autonomous working groups (**A**)?

Possible advantages

	R	L	E	A
● Increased productivity	❑	❑	❑	❑
● Better quality work	❑	❑	❑	❑
● Better relations with customers/clients	❑	❑	❑	❑
● Greater flexibility/adaptability of staff	❑	❑	❑	❑
● Reduced absenteeism	❑	❑	❑	❑
● Better timekeeping	❑	❑	❑	❑
● Lower turnover of staff	❑	❑	❑	❑
● Greater job satisfaction	❑	❑	❑	❑
● Better team morale	❑	❑	❑	❑
● Less need for detailed management/ supervision	❑	❑	❑	❑
● Better relations with management	❑	❑	❑	❑
● Others _____				

Possible disadvantages

	R	L	E	A
● Reduced productivity (at least to begin with)	❑	❑	❑	❑
● Poorer quality work (ditto)	❑	❑	❑	❑
● Increased absenteeism (ditto)	❑	❑	❑	❑
● Poorer timekeeping (ditto)	❑	❑	❑	❑
● Increased turnover of staff (ditto)	❑	❑	❑	❑
● Reduced job satisfaction (ditto)	❑	❑	❑	❑
● Managers' and supervisors' anxieties about their changed roles	❑	❑	❑	❑
● Greater interpersonal conflict	❑	❑	❑	❑
● Poorer team morale	❑	❑	❑	❑
● Increased training costs	❑	❑	❑	❑

	R	L	E	A
● Additional equipment/material costs	❏	❏	❏	❏
● Jobs needing to be regraded and have the pay increased	❏	❏	❏	❏
● Others _____				

_____

There is one basic question in improving people's jobs: how can you help them get what they want out of their jobs, while at the same time ensuring that the organization gets what it wants? But there is no one best answer. It depends entirely on the people and the situation.

> **KEY IDEA**
>
> If you do make an effort to improve people's jobs, make sure you do so only in consultation with the people concerned.

Motivating your team

How can you motivate your staff? That is, how can you get them to work willingly and productively to achieve the results you and the organization want them to achieve? How can you get them to want what you want them to want?

Most of the checklists in this section give guidance that will be helpful in motivating staff. But there are some things that are worth saying separately here.

Over the years there have been many research reports on what motivates people to work. What they seem to boil down to is that people work because they _expect_ to get some sort of rewards from working. And they work harder if they expect that the likelihood, or the amount, of those rewards increases with the quantity or quality of what they produce.

But what sort of rewards are people expecting? There's the difficulty. It's not just money – as so many failed financial incentive schemes have shown. People also value good working conditions and workmates they can get on with, a sense of self-respect or status within the organization, a feeling of having a worthwhile job and of doing it well, and so on.

Furthermore, people differ. Even two people doing the same job may be looking for different rewards from it. Indeed, any individual may now be looking for different rewards from those he or she sought just a few months ago. The effective manager needs to recognize this and to be sensitive to the needs and changing expectations of each *individual* in their team.

So, in order to motivate your staff you need to make sure that they can expect rewards that each one values as a result of their work. Ideally, you should also be able to make sure that increased effort can be expected to result in increased rewards. The following checklists offer some guidance in this.

How is your team's motivation?

Here are the kinds of symptoms that might indicate *poor* motivation. Tick any that are noticeable in your team.

- Low productivity ❏
- Absenteeism ❏
- Poor timekeeping ❏
- High staff turnover ❏
- Poor-quality work ❏
- Customer/client complaints ❏
- Low team morale ❏
- Interpersonal conflicts within team ❏
- Conflicts with management ❏
- Inflexible attitudes to change ❏
- Bad relations with other parts of the organization ❏
- Others _____

Even if none of these symptoms is apparent at present, things can easily change. If one or two individuals get disgruntled, they can often undermine the spirit of the whole team.

What are the rewards?

(a) If you are to maintain or improve the motivation of individuals in your team you need to know what they expect to get out of their work. What does each expect by way of rewards? For example, think of just one individual and, in the column of boxes headed **A**, tick the *three* chief rewards you think that person might be expecting from his or her work.

	A				
– Good wages or salary	❏	❏	❏	❏	❏
– The prospect of promotion	❏	❏	❏	❏	❏
– Official fringe benefits (perks)	❏	❏	❏	❏	❏
– Unofficial fringe benefits	❏	❏	❏	❏	❏
– Getting as much free time as possible	❏	❏	❏	❏	❏
– The satisfaction of turning out high-quality work	❏	❏	❏	❏	❏
– The easy life of undemanding routine work	❏	❏	❏	❏	❏
– The challenge of changing, variable work	❏	❏	❏	❏	❏
– Contributing to a worthwhile enterprise	❏	❏	❏	❏	❏
– Gaining personal status or power	❏	❏	❏	❏	❏
– Agreeable working conditions	❏	❏	❏	❏	❏
– Being told exactly what to do	❏	❏	❏	❏	❏
– Having some freedom to decide how they work	❏	❏	❏	❏	❏
– Getting on well with customers/clients	❏	❏	❏	❏	❏

A

- Social relationships with
  workmates ❑ ❑ ❑ ❑ ❑
- Being respected within the
  organization ❑ ❑ ❑ ❑ ❑
- Being respected by
  outsiders ❑ ❑ ❑ ❑ ❑
- Others _____

_____

(b) Can you now use the *four remaining columns* (and however many more
you need to add) to identify the three chief rewards being expected by
each of the *other* members of your team?

	Yes	No
● Were you able to complete exercises **(a)** and **(b)** above?	❑	❑
● Whether you were or not, do you feel it may be worth trying to think this way about individuals' expectations in the future?	❑	❑
● If you were able to identify rewards for several different individuals, did you decide they would differ at all in what they would find rewarding?	❑	❑
● Are you confident about the rewards you identified with each individual in **(a)** or **(b)** above?	❑	❑
● Can you think of ways in which you might find out *more* about the rewards being enjoyed or expected by different members of your team?	❑	❑
● Can you see ways of arranging for people to obtain and value *new* rewards – ones they are *not* expecting at present (e.g. satisfaction in the work itself)? (See the checklists on **Improving people's jobs**, page 142)	❑	❑

The main point to emerge from this sort of exercise is that team members
may *differ* in the rewards they are seeking. What motivates one may leave
another cold.

Managing the reward system

Even if you know what rewards each individual is seeking, can you use that knowledge to help motivate them? This depends on whether you can convince them that they will get those rewards if they work as you want them to – and only then.

	Yes	No
● Look again at the rewards you have identified for your staff in the list in **(a)** on page 148. Will your staff get any of those rewards (for example, the easy life of undemanding routine work or agreeable working conditions) simply by *keeping* their jobs, rather than by doing them as well as they can?	❏	❏
● If so, is there any way in which you can withhold or alter those rewards so that staff will realize they can get them only by working as you want them to?	❏	❏
● More positively, are there still rewards available that people will value and that can be clearly attached to good performance (rather than just getting by)?	❏	❏
● Can you make it clear to staff (in job descriptions, in objectives and standards, or just in the way you praise or criticize their work) what they have to do to obtain those rewards?	❏	❏

● Finally, can you ensure not just that staff expect to get rewards from working well but also that those who do work well do get the expected rewards? For example, can you:

	Yes	No
– regularly check that each one is satisfied?	❏	❏
– strongly press for well-earned bonuses or pay increases?	❏	❏
– make out strong cases for deserved promotions?	❏	❏
– remove obstacles that prevent people working as well as they wish to?	❏	❏
– protect staff from events or decisions within the organization that might jeopardize their rewards?	❏	❏

	Yes	No
– always make a point of letting people know how pleased you are with their work?	❏	❏
– give new responsibilities to those who want and deserve them?	❏	❏
– keep alert for people's *changing* expectations?	❏	❏
– others _____		

Motivating your team as a whole

Even though individuals are getting the rewards they expect, you may still feel that they are not working together as the coherent team you would like them to be. Which of the following approaches might help you to improve the motivation of your team *as a whole*?

- Make sure that the combined purpose and importance of the team's work is understood by all ❏
- Ensure that the team has discussed and committed itself to the overall tasks or objectives of the group ❏
- Ensure that everyone in the team understands the contribution being made by every other member to the team's tasks or objectives ❏
- Keep the team informed of its progress towards objectives and of its level of performance ❏
- Encourage shared beliefs, values and rewards within the team ❏
- Promote discussion, suggestions and constructive criticism of work practices within the team ❏
- Create a mutually trusting climate in which people are able to express their ideas and feelings without giving offence or offence being taken ❏
- Give the team as much freedom as they can handle in deciding what needs doing and how to do it ❏

- Encourage the team in arriving at consensus decisions rather than allowing bossy individuals to ignore other members' best interests ☐

- Look out for and deal with any jealousies or other conflicts that arise within the team ☐

- Be seen to be a vigorous champion of your team in dealing with people outside it ☐

- Others _____

KEY IDEA

In order to motivate people, find out what rewards they want, lead them to expect those rewards in return for good work and make sure they get them.

Managing conflict

As a manager you are responsible for the activities of your team of people. You may also be working alongside other managers who are responsible for their own teams. As you will be well aware, people don't always see eye to eye. Your team members may fall out among themselves, or with you. They may be at odds with people in other managers' teams. Some may express hostility towards 'the organization'. Managing such conflicts may take up a large slice of your managerial time. It may also present you with some of your most testing and stressful problems.

Conflict is unavoidable in organizations. It is a normal by-product of people trying to work together. Since people differ among themselves you can't expect them to agree all the time. So don't expect to eliminate conflict. Feel satisfied if you can:

- limit the number of outbreaks;
- minimize the scale of each outbreak;
- stop it from spreading too far;

– prevent it from doing irreparable harm to individuals or to the organization (no vendettas) and, where possible;

– make the conflict yield benefits.

The following checklists draw attention to the symptoms and causes of conflict and suggest what you can do to manage it effectively.

Who conflicts with whom?

Think back over the last couple of working weeks. Have you been aware of conflicts:

- Between *you* and:
  - one or more members of your team? ❑
  - one or more members of someone else's team? ❑
  - your manager? ❑
  - another manager? ❑
  - 'the organization'? ❑
- Between members of your team and:
  - other members of your team? ❑
  - members of another team? ❑
  - another manager? ❑
  - the 'organization'? ❑
- Between your manager and his or her manager? ❑
- Between your manager and other managers? ❑
- Other conflicts _____

The symptoms of conflict

Conflict does not always express itself in angry voices and bloodied noses. People who choose to ignore one another are often doing damage to the organization, if not to themselves. Which of the following symptoms do you see in your organization?

- Tears, raised voices, aggressive horseplay, physical fights? ❏
- Statements expressing negative feelings – jealousy, distrust, derision, fear, dislike – about other groups or individuals? ❏
- Individuals being prevented from getting the rewards that are normally given to people who have performed as well as they have? ❏
- People *choosing* not to pass useful information on to others? ❏
- Individuals refusing to talk to one another – or doing so only with, say, icy formality, sarcastic remarks or open aggression? ❏
- People setting up barriers – being unavailable, or approachable only through their own private rules and procedures? ❏
- People being 'off sick' or otherwise absent more frequently than seems normal? ❏
- Low morale and poor productivity, especially if the people concerned blame it on others? ❏

What's caused the conflict?

Even if we recognize the symptoms of conflict between the people we deal with, it's no use trying to tackle the symptoms only. We must look for the underlying cause of the conflict. There are two essential preconditions for conflict:

1 a feeling that things are not (or might cease to be) as one would like them to be;
2 someone (or some group) who can be blamed (or at least punished) for one's dissatisfaction or fear.

So you might ask:

- What dissatisfaction or fear lies behind the individual's hostility?

- Is the other individual or group concerned in the conflict aware of this?

- Does the dissatisfaction or fear really arise from the work situation – or is it a reflection, say, of some family or financial problem brought in from outside?

- Is the individual justified in blaming me or others in the organization for the way he or she feels?

- Is it the case, for example, that individuals are *in competition* for something that *only* one of them can have – e.g. the right to decide how things shall be done, the use of certain resources, or a promotion?

- Are the individuals or groups in conflict with one another because they disagree about:
  - overall goals (i.e. what to measure success by)?
  - priorities (e.g. what to achieve when)?
  - style (e.g. flexibility versus strict rule-following)?
  - which of them has the right to decide certain issues?

- Does the conflict between certain individuals exist not because they are the people they are but because they are in the *roles* they happen to be occupying (e.g. production manager and sales manager)? That is, even if the best of friends were to replace the present individuals in those roles, would they *inevitably* come into conflict because the interests of their groups are different?

Encourage healthy differences

Not all apparent conflict is necessarily harmful. Differences and disagreements can sometimes be beneficial. For example, which of the following have *you* found to be productive in the past?

- The clash of colleagues' opposing viewpoints may stimulate people's creativity. ❏

- A sudden confrontation may reveal why two people have found it difficult to co-operate in the past, and clear the air so that they can get on better in future. ❏

- A brief squabble, if resolved, may be healthier than harbouring suspicion and resentment. ❏

- Antagonists who have fought one another's ideas fairly and cleanly may end up with greater mutual respect. ❏

- Heated debate may be the only way that people can use to provoke one another to reveal where they really stand on certain matters of vital common concern. ❏

- If they are forced to justify their proposals in the face of strong criticism, people may think them through more rigorously first, and implement them more keenly if they are accepted. ❏

- A conflict among some of its members may cause the team to assert its common purpose and so grow in strength. ❏

- A disagreement or dispute may reveal to the manager some basic organizational or job problem that can be put right before more serious trouble occurs. ❏

Preventing conflict

The best way to manage conflict is to prevent it ever arising. You can do this, to some extent, by promoting collaboration and trust within your team – and by preventing any individual from advancing his or her own interests at the expense of other people's. Here are some more specific hints and tips.

- Don't make decisions that will affect people's work without consulting them first.

- Don't criticize anyone's work unless you can make practical suggestions as to how they might improve it.

- Don't make personal attacks on people behind their backs.

- Discourage other people from doing so.

- Don't allow cliques and in-groups to form within your team – especially if they think they are superior and/or want to score off others.

- Reward people for being helpful and supportive to one another.

- Constantly find ways to remind your people that success depends on their being a *team* rather than a collection of individuals.

- Don't act on *assumptions* about how people feel; check with them first.

- Don't back people into corners from which they can't escape without either admitting defeat or escalating the conflict.

- Demonstrate by your own behaviour how disagreements can be resolved without one or both parties being left with bad feelings.

Dealing with conflict

However harmonious the general atmosphere, individuals can still take a dislike to one another. And they can still think that other people are preventing them from getting something they want. So conflicts can still arise. Here are some ways of handling them. Which might have been helpful in the kinds of conflict you've noticed lately?

- Ignore the conflict for a while in the hope that it will all blow over and be forgotten. ❑

- Threaten the conflicting staff with some sort of punishment (or withdrawal of rewards). ❑

- Persuade them to cool their disagreements out of respect for your feelings or the team's harmony. ❑

- Support one side or the other (with or without concessions). ❑

- Impose a compromise. ❑

- Buy people off – 'If you give up fighting for that, I'll give you something else you want instead'. ❑

- Get the rest of the team to gang up and suppress the conflict. ❑

The above approaches sometimes offer short-term relief. But often they merely postpone the day when the conflict re-emerges and has to be dealt with properly. Might you find any of the following approaches more effective?

- Separate conflicting staff so that they are no longer working together. ❑

- If two people are battling for a reward which they believe only one can have, try to find means of enabling *both* to have the reward if they deserve it. ❑

- Help the antagonists to understand one another's point of view and to recognize its validity in the other's eyes. ❑

- Refer the antagonists to some 'ombudsperson' in the organization who is known to provide wise conciliation. ❑

- Persuade the conflicting parties to abandon their pursuit of individual goals in favour of some new, common goal, which both will agree is more important. ❑

- Concentrate on getting the antagonists to work out their own solution rather than pushing your own. ❑

- Negotiate a solution between the antagonists such that *both* can make a satisfactory gain while neither gives up anything he or she regards as essential. ❑

(See the checklists on **Negotiating**, page 38.)

KEY IDEA

The key to resolving conflict is to keep on talking until the antagonists realize that they are more likely to get something worthwhile out of the situation if they work together than if they go on fighting one another.

Counselling your staff

There may be times when you find yourself drawn into counselling a member of staff – perhaps because of problems connected with stress or bullying or harassment, or because the person feels that their career is stagnating. In such cases you will be helping them to solve a problem.

The usual dictionary definition of counselling talks of guidance and advice. Managers have always given guidance and advice, of course, not least in their 'coaching' role. And you will often need to give people clear guidance and advice when you are counselling them. You may even need to take action to solve someone's problem for them – say by separating two work-mates who are not getting on together.

Such a directive approach is not always appropriate. Much in favour nowa-days is the so-called 'client-centred' or 'non-directive' approach. Instead of telling a person how you think they should solve their problem, you let them talk it through, come to terms with it and find *their own* solution. In many cases the person will be unable to 'own' and implement a solution unless it is one they feel they have arrived at for themselves.

As with most management tools there is no one best approach to coun-selling. Both directive and non-directive approaches have advantages in dif-ferent circumstances. You will need to decide which is more appropriate to the problem of the particular person you are counselling.

Preparing for the counselling interview

Don't let yourself get drawn into counselling unexpectedly – or not unless you are sure you have plenty of time, privacy and knowledge about the other person concerned. Otherwise make a date to meet again later, after you have prepared – if indeed you are happy that you are the most appro-priate person to offer the kind of counselling that seems to be needed.

So before you meet the person you'll be counselling, consider the following questions:

	Yes	No
● Do you know, or suspect, what the problem is?	❑	❑
● Does the staff member?	❑	❑
● If not would they recognize that there is a problem?	❑	❑
● Has the staff member indicated a desire for what you regard as counselling?	❑	❑
● If your answer to either or both of the last two questions is 'no', is the staff member likely to be a reluctant interviewee?	❑	❑

	Yes	No

- Have you allowed plenty of time for the interview? ☐ ☐
- Does your staff member know how much time is available? ☐ ☐
- Can you find a place for the interview that is quiet, private and free from interruption? ☐ ☐
- Have you made your staff member aware of the extent to which the discussion can be kept confidential? ☐ ☐
- Is there already some rapport or sense of trust between you and your staff member? ☐ ☐
- If not, is it worth thinking about how you might establish some during the interview? ☐ ☐
- Have you refreshed your memory sufficiently from the personnel files and work records about the person you are going to counsel? ☐ ☐
- Who do you expect to benefit most from the interview:
  - you? ☐
  - the staff member? ☐
  - the team? ☐
  - the organization? ☐
  - customers/clients? ☐
- Do you expect the counselling to be mainly:
  - directive? ☐
  - non-directive? ☐
- Do you believe this is what the staff member expects? ☐ ☐

The process of counselling

Here are some considerations to bear in mind during the interview.

- Have I done all I can to put the other person at his or her ease?
- Have I reminded them how long we have for the discussion?
- Is it necessary for either of us to take notes, or might it be inhibiting?
- What does the other person think?

The agenda

- Have we clarified what the interview is about?
- Have we distinguished between the problem and its symptoms?
- Is there a problem *behind* the problem we are talking about?
- Does the other person recognize the problem?
- Are they expecting me to solve the problem?
- Do I intend to suggest solutions or to help the other person work out their own?
- Which seems more appropriate to me?
- How can I avoid antagonizing the other person if I offer a different approach from what they are expecting?

The discussion

- If I intend being non-directive can I make myself keep quiet and let the other person do most of the talking?
- Can I use open-ended questions (or pauses) to encourage them to say more about issues they introduce hesitantly?
- Can I listen actively and, where appropriate, reflect back what the person is saying to me? (See the checklists on **Listening**, page 209)
- Can I give feedback of a kind that encourages the person to keep talking as long as they need to?
- Am I patient enough to listen to repeated covering of the same ground if it is important to the other person?
- Can I ask for clarification of things I don't understand, without making the person think I am nosey or not paying attention?
- Am I capable of hearing about what the person wants to discuss without showing any discomfort I may feel or making them embarrassed?
- Can I avoid expressing judgements or personal reactions that may make the person watch what they say or even shut up altogether?
- To what extent must I/can I set aside my own values or standards and apply those of the staff member?

- If I have negative feelings towards the other person, can I keep them to myself?
- How far can I accept that the staff member's feelings are as important as the facts of the case?
- Am I on my guard against taking sides in a dispute?
- If the other person makes contradictory statements or statements I believe to be incorrect, will it be more productive to let this pass or to mention how it seems to me?
- If the other person gets defensive about what has happened in the past can I persuade them to start thinking more positively about the future? (Not 'I wish I had . . .' but 'In future I will . . .')
- If they get hostile, can I ease them back on to some common ground where I can be supportive and praising?
- Can I avoid getting hot under the collar (or at least showing it)?
- Can I remember that the purpose of the meeting is not to hand out or take blame but to solve problems?
- Might it be helpful (or would it be counter-productive) to mention any similar problems of my own (or of other people I've known)?
- Am I being careful not to encourage personal confessions that the other person will later regret?
- Will it be helpful to try to summarize the discussion at any point?

Towards a solution

- Do I need to be directive and insist on a particular solution?
- Does the other person need me to suggest some alternative solutions?
- Does it matter to me if the person opts for a solution other than the one I would have chosen?
- Am I required to take some sort of action in helping them implement their solution?
- Do I feel that I need to refer the other person to someone more expert than I am – a doctor, a solicitor, a personnel specialist or whatever?

Evaluating the interview

- Did the other person seem satisfied with the outcome?
- Am I satisfied with the outcome?
- Do we need to meet again?
- Has the other person implemented the solution?
- Does he or she seem happier and/or more productive?
- Does the improvement last?
- What have I learned about the counselling process?
- Do I need briefing or training to help me be more effective in a counselling role?

N.B. You may find it useful also to look at the checklist on 'Questioning techniques' in **Selection interviewing** (page 126), at **The interview in staff appraisal** (page 168) and the checklists on **Listening** (page 209).

> **KEY IDEA**
>
> Don't despair if you feel you've talked at length about a person's problem without having reached a solution – the opportunity to talk at length sometimes IS the solution.

Running a staff appraisal system

Your organization, like many others nowadays, may have some kind of system for formally appraising and perhaps reporting on the work of staff. Usually this is done once a year, though six-monthly appraisals are not unknown. If your organization does have such a system you will be expected to fit in with it, both by having your own work appraised by your manager and by appraising the work of the staff you are responsible for. If there is no such formal system within the organization, you may need to consider whether something of the sort might be worth introducing in your section.

As an effective manager you will, of course, be appraising the work of your staff continually but informally day by day or week by week throughout the year. Without such regular informal appraisal there would be no way of ensuring that the section's work was running according to plan. (See the checklists on **Controlling**, page 71.)

The formal annual appraisal gives you and your staff a different kind of opportunity. It allows you to look back over the previous months and to consider the appraisals you have made (and each staff member's responses to them) *as a whole*.

What might this tell you about the developing strengths or lingering weaknesses of each individual? What does the staff member see when looking back over his or her year's work? How do you both feel about it? What can be done to build on the individual's strengths and overcome any weaknesses, or remove any difficulties, that prevent them achieving all that they might? How might you expect the person to develop, or what might you expect them to attain, by the time of the *next* formal appraisal?

Maybe you'll want to start thinking about developing a system of your own, if your organization does not already have one, that will help you make such managerial decisions. The following checklists should give you guidance whatever the system.

Do you have a system?

● What kind of appraisal system operates in your organization? (More than one of the following statements may apply.)
  – A formal system which all managers are required to operate ❑
  – Reports to be written on all staff ❑
  – All staff to be *offered* an appraisal interview ❑
  – All staff to be given an appraisal interview whether they want it or not ❑
  – Different systems operate at different levels ❑
  – I am appraised differently from my staff ❑
  – There is no formal appraisal system ❑
  – I am free to appraise as I think fit ❑

- Here are some of the reasons commonly given for staff
  appraisal. Whether or not you run such a system at
  present, which of them would you most look for in
  appraising your own staff? (Again, more than one of
  them may apply.)
  - To agree on just what a person's job actually consists
    of   ❏
  - To assess a person's past performance in the job   ❏
  - To assess future potential in the job   ❏
  - To assess potential in other jobs   ❏
  - To pick out those who might benefit from a change
    of job   ❏
  - To pick out those worthy of promotion or special pay
    awards   ❏
  - To identify individuals' strengths and weaknesses   ❏
  - To identify difficulties that prevent people from
    working as effectively as they might   ❏
  - To consider how individuals might benefit from
    training   ❏
  - To influence their work by praise or advice   ❏
  - To enable staff members to put their point of view
    and influence my expectations   ❏
  - To ensure that I really do think systematically about
    each individual's performance at least once a year   ❏

N.B. The chief emphasis in most appraisal schemes these days is on helping individuals improve their performance in their present jobs.

- What factors do you take into account in appraising staff?
  (Or what factors would you *expect* to take into account if
  you are thinking of setting up an appraisal system?) Tick
  as many as apply.
  - Performance against objectives or targets previously
    agreed with each staff member   ❏
  - Performance against objectives or targets imposed by
    management   ❏
  - Standards of performance previously agreed with each
    staff member   ❏

- Standards imposed by management ❏
- 'Critical incidents', e.g. regular events in the work that test a person's skills to the full ❏
- Personal qualities or attitudes revealed in the person's work ❏
- Other people's comments on the person ❏
- Others _____

	Yes	No
Can you be sure you are appraising the individual's performance rather than your idea of his or her personality?	❏	❏
Does your memory or record-keeping enable you to base the appraisal on the *whole* period under review, rather than on the recent past or on a few outstanding but untypical events?	❏	❏
Does your appraisal system involve the filling in of one or more reporting *forms*?	❏	❏
If so, are you confident about what is required of you in filling in such forms?	❏	❏
Are you expected to interview your staff?	❏	❏
If so, do you feel sufficiently confident about such interviewing?	❏	❏
In general, do you feel you know all you need to know about the purpose and workings of your appraisal system?	❏	❏
If not, how can you learn more? _____		

The staff member's involvement

The checklists above reflect the manager's angle on staff appraisal. But what about the individuals being appraised? What do they expect from it?

How can they get the most out of it?

● What might your staff members be hoping to get from an appraisal?
  (Think about the last appraisal you had, if any, from your own
  manager.) Might they hope:
  – for a chance to redefine their own responsibilities? ❏
  – to find out how they are seen to be doing? ❏
  – to discuss problems in the job situation? ❏
  – to put forward ideas for improving their job? ❏
  – to get praise for work well done? ❏
  – to get constructive criticisms of weaknesses? ❏
  – to agree on a plan for the year ahead? ❏
  – to discuss the possible need for a change of job? ❏
  – to make a case for extra pay or promotion? ❏
  – to discuss training needs and agree action on them? ❏
  – to learn more about you? ❏
  – to learn more about the policies and problems of the
    section or organization? ❏
  – to put forward their own suggestions for improving
    the effectiveness of the section or organization? ❏
  – to seek counselling on matters that may or may not
    be closely connected with their job performance? ❏
  – others _____
    _____

● Clearly, formal appraisal *can* give useful opportunities to
  the person being appraised as well as to the manager. But
  are people encouraged to make maximum use of this
  opportunity? For example, are staff in your scheme:
  – aware of when the appraisal will be carried out? ❏
  – aware of what form it will take? ❏
  – encouraged to prepare for the appraisal? ❏
  – asked to contribute some kind of self-appraisal? ❏
  – asked to make other comments or suggestions about
    their jobs or the work of the section? ❏
  – told what the appraiser has said about them? ❏

– given the opportunity to comment on or contest the
appraisal? ❏

– involved in making whatever decisions may arise out
of the appraisal? ❏

– offered an interview with the appraiser and/or with
someone more senior? ❏

– shown and perhaps given a copy of any written report
that results from the appraisal? ❏

● If staff members are not fully involved in each of the
ways listed above is there any compelling reason why
not? Is it time the system was changed?

The interview in staff appraisal

Many managers feel uncomfortable about conducting appraisal interviews.
Certainly there are several potential problems in doing so. Which of the following have you come across (or might you expect) with your staff?

● Staff member's reluctance to be interviewed ❏

● My uncertainty as to the purpose of interview ❏

● Artificiality of the situation ❏

● My expectations of the interview are very different from
those of the staff member ❏

● My appraisal of his or her performance comes as a big
shock to the staff member ❏

● Lack of ideas as to how a person might be helped to
improve his or her performance ❏

● Dealing with people who are not outstandingly good or
bad but just mediocre in performance ❏

● Finding something motivating to say to people who have
got as far as they are likely to get ❏

● Handling staff who think they ought to be rising faster
(or in different directions) than I do ❏

- Disagreements with other managers (especially my own manager) about some people's performance ❑

Preparing to interview

If you need to interview staff as part of the appraisal process, it is worth thinking about how you might prepare for the interview, how you might carry it out, and how you might follow it up afterwards.

- For each individual member of staff, what might be your main *purposes* in the interview? (See the list of reasons given for staff appraisal on page 165.)

- What *information* about the person might you need or wish to have before the interview? For example:
  - details of their performance since the last appraisal ❑
  - details of their actual duties ❑
  - their workplan/objectives (if any) for the year in question ❑
  - notes of any problems or difficulties ❑
  - their strengths ❑
  - their weaknesses ❑
  - any training they have had during the year ❑
  - their ambitions or expectations ❑

- Which of the following sources might be useful to you in gathering the information you need?
  - The person's job description ❑
  - Any records you have of their work performance over the year ❑
  - Notes of any occasions on which you have had to single them out for special praise or reprimand ❑
  - The record of the last appraisal interview ❑
  - Other records/reports _____ ❑
  - The individual ❑
  - Your own manager ❑
  - Other people who know the person ❑

- How long will you allow for each interview? _____

- For each member of staff, what are the main points you would want to cover under each of the following three main headings?
  - Introduction _____

    _____
  - Main body of the interview _____

    _____
  - Conclusion _____

    _____

- Try to ensure that the person you are interviewing *also* prepares for the interview, either by filling out some standard self-appraisal form or by working through a checklist such as this:
  - **(a)** *Think about your past year's work:*
    - What have you done that has given you most satisfaction?
    - What are you least satisfied about?
    - In what ways (if any) has your job changed over the year?
    - Have you met any big obstacles or problems?
  - **(b)** *Think about possible improvements:*
    - What might you do to become more effective over the coming year?
    - What obstacles/problems might we be able to lessen or remove?
    - How might the job be changed to help you to become more effective?
  - **(c)** *Think about plans for the year ahead:*
    - What tasks do you expect to perform in the year ahead?
    - What objectives/goals/targets/deadlines do you expect to have to reach?
    - What additional support, resources or training do you think you might need?
  - **(d)** *Any other matters you want to raise?*

Carrying out the interview

Here is one possible sequence for an appraisal interview. Add, delete or change around any items to suit your own needs.

1 Put the staff member at ease.

2 Remind him/her of the purpose and potential benefits of the interview.

3 Discuss and give praise for his or her strengths and achievements over the year.

4 Explore any areas of weakness or underachievement.

5 Invite the staff member to consider such weaknesses as problems you may be able to solve by sharing ideas.

6 Ask about the person's ideas for change and improvement, and discuss them in relation to your own.

7 Consider what changes might be made in the year ahead and agree on a workplan, perhaps setting objectives or targets.

8 Broaden the discussion by encouraging the staff member to raise any worries, hopes or ambitions that have not been mentioned so far.

9 Discuss these as helpfully as possible and consider what further action you or the staff member might usefully take.

10 Conclude the interview by summarizing what you have both agreed to do as a result.

Here are a few further questions to remind you of appropriate approaches during the interview.

- Am I encouraging the other person to regard the interview as a *two-way* exchange of ideas? ❏

- Have I found out what he/she wants to discuss? ❏

- Are we giving it adequate attention? ❏

- Am I managing to avoid coming across as an interrogator? ❏

- Am I asking the kinds of questions ('open' questions) that encourage the other person to reflect on their work? ❏

- Am I patient enough to leave pauses that allow them time for reflection and considered answers? ❏

- Am I really listening to what the other person is saying (rather than thinking about what I plan to say next)? ❏

- Am I open to hearing about their feelings and anxieties without myself getting upset? ❏

- Am I responding positively and supportively enough to what I hear? ❏

- Can I get the interviewee to mention any weaknesses or performance shortcomings that I want to discuss? ❏

- Can I get him or her to think of these as a problem that we can try to solve together (rather than as personal failings that I want to blame them for)? ❏

- Can I sufficiently involve the interviewee in analyzing the problem situation so that we emerge with a 'solution' we can both accept as 'ours'? ❏

- Am I scrupulous about dealing with the person as an individual rather than acting as though everyone of their age, sex, race, background, etc. were the same? ❏

- By the end of the interview have we reached an understanding that is realistic and acceptable to me, to the interviewee and to the organization? ❏

You may find it helpful to look at the checklists on 'Conducting the interview' in **Selection interviewing** (page 126) and at the checklists on **Listening** (page 209) and **Counselling your staff** (page 158).

Following up on the interview

What do you need to do once the interview is over?

- Make a note of the main points discussed and of whatever action you and the interviewee agreed. ❏

- Ensure that the interviewee gets a copy. ❏

- Send on whatever paperwork is required by, for example, your manager or the personnel section. ❏

- Do whatever it was you promised the interviewee you would do to help them. ❏

- Ensure that they do whatever they promised to do.   ❑

- Anything else _____

_____

KEY IDEA

Staff appraisal should not be a once-a-year ritual. Good managers do it all
the year round.

Disciplining staff

Most managers hate having to take formal disciplinary action against their
staff. They suspect, usually quite rightly, that their superiors will think it
signifies some sort of failure on the manager's part. Did they select the
wrong people in the first place? Did they fail to set them appropriate tasks?
Did they fail to motivate them or give them proper leadership? And, above
all, why couldn't they have sorted out the problem informally – with a few
firm but reasonable words in the ear of the individual concerned – rather
than letting it blow up into formal procedures? (See the checklists on **Motivating your team**, page 146, **Developing leadership**, page 195 and **Counselling your staff**, page 158). Besides, the thought of having to justify their
actions to their managers, let alone to an industrial tribunal, is enough to
put many managers off 'making it official'.

Nevertheless, even the best of managers will sometimes find certain individuals very difficult to deal with. Such individuals just don't respond to
your informal comments and friendly criticisms, however often you repeat
them. They need to have it spelled out to them, in writing if necessary – and
be told what will happen to them if they don't improve. And it is important
to do this sooner rather than later. If you let people get away with unacceptable behaviour or poor productivity for too long it may:

- undermine your authority;

- demoralise the rest of your staff;

- prevent your taking effective action later on;

- irritate your manager and fellow managers;

– alienate clients or customers;

– do damage to your organization.

If you absolutely must take disciplinary action, it is essential to do so with irreproachable care and fairness. That is why the following checklists, which give the necessary guidance, need to be particularly detailed.

The disciplinary procedures of your organization

If and when you do find it necessary to formally discipline a member of staff you must be seen to act in a way that:

– encourages the individual to improve (unless the offence is so serious that dismissal is called for);

– is fair and reasonable (see the checklists on **Managing equal opportunities**, page 84);

– is the same for all such offenders; and

– follows procedures that all employees are fully aware of.

Otherwise you may find your decision being overturned by your higher management or by an industrial tribunal.

	Yes	No
● Does your organization have a formal written procedure for disciplining staff?	❏	❏
● If trade unions are recognized by the organization, has the procedure been accepted by them?	❏	❏
● If it has not, how are their objections handled? _____		

_____

● How far is your organization's formal procedure in line with the suggestions made (in the UK) by the Arbitration and Conciliation Advisory Service (ACAS)? Tick those that apply in the following list. ACAS suggests that procedures should:
  – be in writing; ❏
  – specify to whom they apply; ❏

- provide for matters to be dealt with quickly; ❏
- specify what disciplinary actions may be taken; ❏
- say which levels of management have authority to take which disciplinary actions; ❏
- provide for individuals to be informed of the complaint against them and be given an opportunity to put their point of view before decisions are made; ❏
- give individuals the right to be accompanied at disciplinary discussions by a trade union representative or a fellow employee of their choice; ❏
- ensure that, except for gross misconduct, employees cannot be dismissed on first formal notice of a breach of discipline; ❏
- ensure that no disciplinary penalties are imposed until the case has been fully investigated; ❏
- ensure that individuals are given an explanation for any penalty imposed; ❏
- provide a right of appeal and state the procedure to be followed. ❏

Informing your staff about discipline

	Yes	No
Do all members of staff receive a copy of the formal procedure?	❏	❏
If not, do they know where they can easily see a copy?	❏	❏
Is the procedure clearly worded so that all members of staff, including you, are sure what is intended?	❏	❏
Are all members of staff issued with a copy of any rules of the organization?	❏	❏
If not, are copies displayed in places where staff cannot avoid seeing them?	❏	❏
Are the rules clearly worded so that there can be no argument as to what is intended?	❏	❏

	Yes	No
• Have you made clear to staff any rules that apply especially in your section?	❏	❏
• Have you made all members of your staff aware of what you expect from them as a reasonable job performance?	❏	❏

Before you discipline an individual

Here are the questions to ask yourself before deciding to call someone for a formal disciplinary interview.

	Yes	No
• Am I absolutely sure that an offence has been committed?	❏	❏
• Is the offence one of:		
– misconduct?	❏	❏
– poor job performance?	❏	❏
– both?	❏	❏
• Could the person have been *unaware* that he/she was committing an offence?	❏	❏
• If misconduct took place away from work, does it still come under the disciplinary procedure?	❏	❏
• How convinced am I that the person committed the offence:		
– do I have evidence (or merely suspicions)?	❏	❏
– is the evidence direct (or merely hearsay)?	❏	❏
– how far can I trust the bearers of hearsay?	❏	❏
– even if an offence was committed, can I be sure who committed it?	❏	❏
– would my 'evidence' stand up to cross-examination in a public hearing (e.g. in an industrial tribunal)?	❏	❏
• If the person does appear to have committed an offence, are there any *extenuating circumstances*? For example:		
– was the individual aware of the expected job performance?	❏	❏

	Yes	No
– was this expressed in terms that leave no room for doubt in terms of quantities or time?	❏	❏
– was it reasonable to expect such a performance from this particular person?	❏	❏
– has the person had appropriate training?	❏	❏
– has the person had appropriate support from other staff or from equipment and materials?	❏	❏
– is the individual suffering from personal or medical problems?	❏	❏
– does the offence mark a departure from the person's normal standards of conduct or performance? (If so, why?)	❏	❏
– have I or other managers turned a blind eye to this person behaving in this way in the past?	❏	❏
– have other members of staff committed similar offences and not been disciplined?	❏	❏
– does the individual claim innocence or extenuating circumstances?	❏	❏

- Is the alleged offence one that the organization regards as gross misconduct? For example:

	Yes	No
– stealing the organization's money?	❏	❏
– stealing valuable property or materials?	❏	❏
– defrauding the organization?	❏	❏
– stealing from fellow employees?	❏	❏
– dealing dishonestly with customers/clients?	❏	❏
– sexually harassing fellow employees?	❏	❏
– violating equal opportunities policy?	❏	❏
– maliciously damaging the organization's property?	❏	❏
– physically assaulting other employees?	❏	❏
– flagrantly refusing to be bound by the terms of contract?	❏	❏

- If so, must the individual be dealt with differently from people accused of less serious offences – e.g. by being suspended on full pay while the matter is investigated or by being interviewed by a manager senior to yourself? ❏ ❏

Setting up a disciplinary interview

- How quickly can/must I call the interview after first noticing the offence? (The quicker the better.) _____

  _____

- How do I make clear to the individual that this is to be a disciplinary interview (as laid down in the formal procedure) – and not just an informal pep-talk? _____

  _____

- Who will be present at the interview besides me and the individual? For example:

	Yes	No
– my manager?	❏	❏
– another manager?	❏	❏
– my bodyguard?	❏	❏
– the individual's union representative?	❏	❏
– a fellow employee of his or her choice?	❏	❏

- Do I have all the necessary paperwork to hand? For example:

	Yes	No
– the individual's personal file?	❏	❏
– a copy of the rules that have been broken?	❏	❏
– a written statement as to what is alleged to have happened, together with the evidence supporting this allegation?	❏	❏
– the person's job description or workplan (if any)?	❏	❏
– records indicating the person's inadequate job performance (time sheets, sales figures, customer complaints, etc.)?	❏	❏
– comparative records for other staff – especially those with whom the individual is most likely to compare his or her conduct or job performance?	❏	❏
– copies of letters, memos, etc. concerning the person's case?	❏	❏

	Yes	No

- What is my *prime* purpose in calling the interview?
  For example:
  - to help the person to improve? (This should be paramount where it is still a realistic possibility.)   ❑ ❑
  - to set an example to other members of my staff?   ❑ ❑
  - to set an example to other managers?   ❑ ❑
  - to publicize my high standards?   ❑ ❑
  - to begin dismissal procedures – for an individual who has failed to respond to previous warnings or who has committed 'gross misconduct'?   ❑ ❑
- Prior to the interview, shall I give the person a *written* note of the precise nature of the misconduct or poor performance that I wish to discuss?   ❑ ❑

At the disciplinary interview

	Yes	No

- At the interview, shall I give the person the opportunity to:
  - ask for further details of the alleged offence?   ❑ ❑
  - consider the evidence?   ❑ ❑
  - dispute it where necessary?   ❑ ❑
  - present alternative evidence?   ❑ ❑
  - refute, explain or justify the alleged offence?   ❑ ❑
- How can I give the person (and/or the person's companion) maximum opportunity to present the best case possible – for example by:
  - allowing plenty of time?   ❑ ❑
  - asking 'open-ended questions' (see the checklist on 'questioning techniques' in **Selection interviewing**, page 126) to encourage the individual to talk freely?   ❑ ❑
  - letting the individual do most of the talking?   ❑ ❑

	Yes	No

    – avoiding giving the impression that I have already decided how blameworthy the person is and/or what form the penalty must take? ☐ ☐

● Does it now appear that the alleged offence did NOT take place – or that there were extenuating circumstances (see the checklist on *extenuating circumstances* on page 176)? ☐ ☐

● Do I decide my 'verdict' here and now, and let the individual know immediately? ☐ ☐

● Do I decide the *penalty* (if any) here and now, and tell the individual immediately? ☐ ☐

● What will be the chief purpose of the penalty? (See the alternatives in the checklist on page 179.) _____

_____

● What form of penalty shall I apply. For example:
    – a formal *oral* warning (for a minor offence)? ☐ ☐
    – a formal *written* warning (for a serious, or repeated minor, offence)? ☐ ☐
    – a *final* written warning? ☐ ☐
    – suspension (with or without pay)? ☐ ☐
    – transfer to another part of the organization? ☐ ☐
    – dismissal with due notice or with pay in lieu of notice? ☐ ☐
    – instant dismissal? ☐ ☐

● In telling the person about the penalty, do I:
    – insist on the presence of a trade union representative or other colleague? ☐ ☐
    – explain the reason for the penalty? ☐ ☐
    – outline what disciplinary steps would need to be taken should the person commit further offences? ☐ ☐
    – explain the person's right of appeal (if any)? ☐ ☐
    – confirm all the above in writing? ☐ ☐

● How do I make clear what is expected from the person if he or she is to stay out of disciplinary trouble in future? _____

Issuing a warning

	Yes	No

- If I am issuing a warning, shall I make clear:
  - the nature of the offence? ☐ ☐
  - the standard of behaviour required in future? ☐ ☐
  - any support or training that will be given to help the person attain the required standard? ☐ ☐
  - the further penalty that will result if the individual misbehaves or fails to reach the standard within a specified period of time? ☐ ☐

- When I am issuing a formal *oral* warning for what I believe to be a *first* offence, shall I also:
  - check whether a previous oral warning has been issued recently? ☐ ☐
  - record it in the individual's personal file? ☐ ☐
  - make clear to the individual that this is part of the organization's formal disciplinary procedure? ☐ ☐

- When I am issuing a *written* warning for a serious or repeated offence, or a *final* warning if a written warning has already been issued, shall I:
  - check first with higher management? ☐ ☐
  - ask the person to sign a copy as evidence of having received it? ☐ ☐
  - provide a copy for a trade union representative? ☐ ☐
  - tell the person about any right of appeal? ☐ ☐

- What action does my organization's disciplinary procedure require me to take if further offences occur after a warning has been issued and within a reasonable or specified period of time?

- Do I delete all mention of warnings from an individual's personal file if there has been no repetition of offences within a certain period of time – six months, one year, two years or whatever? ☐ ☐

Dismissing an employee

If the person must be dismissed:

	Yes	No
• Am I quite certain that the disciplinary procedure has been followed precisely?	❏	❏
• Have I checked on any trade union action that may follow?	❏	❏
• Do I allow the person to work out his or her contractual notice?	❏	❏
• Or do I ask him/her to go immediately with pay in lieu of notice?	❏	❏
• Have I informed the person of any right of appeal against the decision?	❏	❏
• Am I sure that the person will have no effective case to take to an industrial tribunal?	❏	❏
• Have I kept my manager and/or higher management fully informed?	❏	❏
• Am I sure of their backing?	❏	❏
• If I intend the dismissal to be *summary/instant* (that is, without notice or payment in lieu of notice), am I totally convinced that:		
– the person has committed gross misconduct?	❏	❏
– the person could have been in no doubt that he/she was committing gross misconduct?	❏	❏
– the person could have been in no doubt that the misconduct would make him/her liable for summary dismissal?	❏	❏
– there were no extenuating circumstances?	❏	❏
– comparable misconduct has not been ignored by management in the recent past?	❏	❏
– the case has been fully and fairly investigated?	❏	❏
– the decision has been arrived at coolly, perhaps after an appropriate delay for second thoughts?	❏	❏

	Yes	No
– approval has been given at the highest necessary level of management?	❑	❑

N.B. If an individual is to be summarily dismissed, do not make any payments in lieu of notice. To do so might compromise your position, should the case come before an industrial tribunal.

Appeals

	Yes	No
● Do you know your organization's appeals procedure (if any exists)?	❑	❑
● Could you make the appeals procedure clear to any individual you are disciplining in accordance with (in the UK) the Employment Protection (Consolidation) Act of 1978?	❑	❑
● If individuals have a right of appeal, do they know:		
– to whom the appeal should be addressed?	❑	❑
– in what form to make the appeal?	❑	❑
– the time limit within which they must appeal?	❑	❑
● Are all such details given in any written warning or dismissal notice?	❑	❑

Following up on the procedure

	Yes	No
● Have you ensured that all written evidence you have collected, together with any notes you may have made during the disciplinary interview, have been put into the individual's personal file?	❑	❑
● In so far as the purpose of your disciplinary action was to encourage the person to *improve*, have you decided precisely what you will be looking out for (and when) in the weeks to come?	❑	❑

	Yes	No
● Have you taken steps to provide the person with whatever training or support he/she needs in order to improve?	❏	❏
● Have you made a note in your diary to review the individual's progress by the end of a certain reasonable period?	❏	❏
● Will you remember to delete from the individual's personal file all reference to the earlier warning if and when this becomes appropriate?	❏	❏
● If it has been necessary to dismiss a member of your team, will you be able to explain this to the rest of the team in such a way as to avoid damaging morale?	❏	❏

KEY IDEA

In no other area of management is it so necessary to 'go by the book'. Fail to follow the set procedures and, however justified your reason for getting rid of an unproductive or disruptive member of staff, you could find your decision being overturned.

CHAPTER FIVE

Managing information

Contents

Introduction

Information is the life-blood of any operation. Unless you get hold of the right information at the right time, you won't know what's going on. You won't be able to plan and make appropriate decisions. And, unless you send out the right information at the right time (and in the right way to the right individuals or groups), you won't get people to carry out your intentions. Your operation won't know where to go and will have no means of getting anywhere.

Ours has sometimes been called 'the age of information' and certainly many of us feel as if we are drowning in the stuff. We are bombarded with information day and night – in conversations, in written material, on computer screens, on radio and television. Information overload can cause us to tune out and stop paying attention. But we cannot afford to ignore it all. Indeed we may need to go looking for more. Some of that information is directed at us personally and much that isn't can also be turned to our advantage – especially when we turn it into information that we ourselves want to communicate.

Part of your job of managing an operation will be handling the communication of information – both inwards and outwards. You will need to gather appropriate information from members of your team and from sources outside it. You will need to communicate your own decisions, plans and suggestions as information for other people to respond to.

The checklists in this section are concerned with how information is communicated. They should help you to develop your competence both as a gatherer or receiver of information and also as a sender of information. In addition, they should help you review your information needs and consider how best to improve your approaches to obtaining, recording and using information.

Communicating

Managers must communicate. Communication is about conveying our ideas and feelings to one another. We do this because we want to influence one another's understanding, attitudes or actions.

Without such communication, group work would be impossible. Unless we were able to *share* ideas and feelings, each of us would have to act as an isolated individual. Each would have to go his or her own way – without influence or advice from others. We survive by sharing information.

Communication is a two-way process. (Otherwise it might just as well be called 'munication'!) You are not just a sender of information to other people. You are also the target and – if you are paying attention – the receiver of other people's information. Communication implies some sort of scope for *dialogue*.

The checklists that follow invite you to think about:

– with whom you have to communicate;

– why you need to communicate;

– which forms of communication to use;

– what hinders your communication;

– how you might improve communication.

With whom do you communicate?

Until they stop and think about it, many managers are scarcely aware of just how many different people they do communicate with. (They will probably also be communicating with these different people for different purposes and using different approaches.)

● For instance, tick whichever of the following you have communicated with (face to face, in writing or on the telephone) during the last working week:
  – your manager   ❑
  – your manager's manager   ❑
  – fellow managers in your organization   ❑
  – consultants or advisors (internal or external)   ❑
  – your team members   ❑
  – people they are responsible for (if any)   ❑
  – other managers' team members   ❑

- job applicants ❑
- union representatives ❑
- customers or clients ❑
- suppliers ❑
- competitors ❑
- professional acquaintances in other organizations ❑
- press, radio or TV representatives ❑
- others _____

_____

- Which did you communicate with most often? _____

_____

Why do you communicate?

We communicate in order to convey information – ideas or feelings, or both. But why? Usually we do it in order to *influence* the way other people see things or do things. So it is always worth asking what *purpose* lies behind any act of communication – your's or someone else's.

For example, which of the following purposes of communication have cropped up in your own recent work? Tick any you recognize. And can you see any that are specially relevant to each of the people you've ticked in the list above?

- Giving people information on which they can act or not act as they see fit ❑
- Receiving such information from other people ❑
- Seeking information – actively encouraging people to tell you things they might otherwise have kept to themselves ❑
- Having information sought from you ❑
- Giving people information or instructions – on which you expect them to act in a way acceptable to you ❑
- Receiving such information or instructions on which *you* are expected to act according to someone else's expectations ❑

- Motivating/persuading/encouraging – where you expect to meet some resistance, tiredness, or lack of confidence or stamina in the person concerned ❏
- Receiving such motivation/persuasion/encouragement ❏
- Praising, reassuring, expressing interest in someone – or otherwise indicating that you feel well disposed towards them ❏
- Receiving the previous kind of communication from other people ❏
- Criticizing, blaming or otherwise making clear that you feel badly about someone and/or about their work ❏
- Receiving the previous kind of communication from other people ❏
- Others _____

Often when you speak to someone you will have *more than one* of these purposes in mind. But it's still worth asking what is your *main* purpose. What effect, if any, are you hoping to have on the thoughts, feelings or actions of the person you are communicating with?

Equally you might ask the same of anyone who communicates with you. Why are they doing it? What, if anything, do they expect of you? Watch out for 'mixed messages' and 'hidden agendas'. Are they, for instance, giving you information in order to help your decision-making, to force you to act in a certain way, to make you think well of them, to cheer you up, to get you off their backs, to mislead you or what?

How do you communicate?

We communicate information in many different ways. Chiefly we use words, spoken or written. But we also convey ideas and feelings through our *actions* (or lack of them) and through the *image* of ourselves we present to other people. Similarly we learn about other people's ideas and feelings through such 'non-verbal communication' – but very often neither senders nor receivers are consciously aware that any communication is taking place!

Which of the following forms of communication do you use in the course of a normal working week?

Spoken words

- Informal face-to-face conversation with an individual ❏
- More formal one-to-one interviewing ❏
- Formal interviewing as a member of a panel ❏
- Informal group conversation ❏
- More formal group discussions/meetings ❏
- A presentation to a formal gathering ❏
- Telephone conversation with an individual ❏
- Voice mail ❏
- Group telephone discussion using 'conference calls' ❏
- Video conferencing ❏
- Others _____

Written materials

- Writing e-mails, memos and letters ❏
- Reading e-mails, memos and letters ❏
- Writing reports or discussion documents ❏
- Reading reports or discussion documents ❏
- Producing financial or statistical data ❏
- Interpreting financial or statistical data ❏
- Writing notices for noticeboards ❏
- Reading notices on noticeboards ❏
- Writing articles for in-house journals, newsletters, etc. ❏
- Reading other people's articles ❏
- Writing suggestions for a suggestions box ❏

- Reading other people's suggestions ❑
- Writing articles for professional/trade journals ❑
- Reading other people's journal articles ❑
- Sharing information on the Internet ❑
- Others _____

Non-verbal communication

People are usually less aware of their non-verbal communication. But we all do communicate not just in the words we speak but also with the way that we speak them. We also 'say' things without using words at all. For instance, which of the following do you agree might convey ideas and feelings – either to you from others or from you to them?

- Tone of voice (e.g. friendly or sarcastic) ❑
- Accent (e.g. regional or 'BBC' in the UK) ❑
- Pitch of voice (e.g. high or deep) ❑
- Speaking speed (e.g. rapid or leisurely) ❑
- People's use of silence in conversations ❑
- Facial expressions and/or hand gestures ❑
- Body language – the way people sit or stand, or move about, or look us in the eye (or don't) ❑
- People's choice of clothes, cars, office decor, friends, diet, lifestyle, etc. ❑
- Personal habits (e.g. cleanliness, promptness at meetings, etc.) ❑
- Others _____

Much of the information we pick up from such non-verbal communication is not very specific. You just get feelings about the other person, often without realizing why, and certainly without evaluating how far they are relevant to what the person thinks he or she is trying to tell us. Likewise we are often not aware of our own non-verbal messages – or of the image we thus present to other people.

What hinders your communication?

As a manager you'll be only too aware that communication often fails. There are several reasons why people may fail to share their ideas and feelings as effectively as might be desired.

Which of the following barriers to effective communication seem common in *your* organization?

- Lack of clarity in the message – e.g. because the senders aren't sure why they are sending it, or because they don't wish to be clearly understood ❑

- Faulty presentation – e.g. giving complicated information face-to-face when it should have been written down, or overloading a report with irritating jargon ❑

- Incapacity of the receiver – the person receiving the message may lack the sense (or maybe just the background knowledge) to see the point of it ❑

- Mistaken meanings – the sender and receiver of the message may understand it differently and thus be at cross purposes ❑

- Incompatible viewpoints – the sender and receiver (like, say, production and sales staff) may see the world so differently that common understanding is difficult to achieve ❑

- Interpersonal feelings – if people have strong feelings about one another (approving or disapproving) these may affect how they understand (or misunderstand) the message ❑

- Deception – communication sometimes fails because people issue 'disinformation' (tell plausible lies) in order to achieve their own hidden purposes ❑

- Interference – distractions, such as noise, heat, anxiety, ill health, poor light, etc., may cause a message to be misheard or misread ❑

- Lack of channels – your organization may simply have no means of enabling contact between people who need certain kinds of information and the people who have it ❑

- Build-up of distortion – the longer the chain of people along which a message must pass (as in the game of Chinese whispers), the more likely it is to be garbled by the time it reaches those at the end ❑

- Others _____

How to improve communication

Here are two checklists that will help you to improve communication – first as the sender of messages, and secondly as the intended target and receiver of messages.

As sender

Here are the questions to ask yourself.

- Have I identified (all) the most *appropriate* target(s)?

- What do I want my target to understand, believe, and above all **do** as a result of my communication?

- What exactly do I need to say to have this effect on my target?

- What is the most appropriate *medium* – speech, face to face, telephone or writing – for getting my message received and understood by my target?

- What do I have to do to make *effective* use of that medium of communication?

- What potential *barriers* to communication (see opposite) do I foresee between me and the target?

- How can I *minimize* or overcome them?

- What kind of *feedback* shall I expect from the target to convince me that my message has been received and understood?

- Am I ready to respond if my target wants to become a sender and give *me* a message?

As target

Here are the questions to ask yourself when someone is opening up a communication with you.

- Is the sender right in identifying *me* as a target for his/her message?
- What *effect* does the sender want to have on my understanding, attitudes, behaviour – what am I expected to do as a result?
- What *message* does the sender apparently want to convey? (For example, could I restate it to his/her satisfaction?)
- Am I allowing any of the common *barriers to communication* to spoil my understanding?
- Is there any *hidden agenda* of meaning that I am expected to respond to?
- Is the sender telling me the *truth*, the whole truth and nothing but the truth (as far as he or she knows it)?
- Even if the sender *believes* the information to be true, how far can I rely on his or her judgement?
- Is the sender conveying any *unintended* messages (perhaps non-verbally) that I need to take note of?
- What kind of *feedback* does the sender need from me to show that the message has been received and understood?
- Do I need to ask the sender to *clarify* or expand on the message?
- As well as acknowledging receipt of the message, do I need to become a sender myself and return a message of *my own*?

You must already be pretty skilled at communication to have become a manager in the first place. But there is always more to learn. There are certainly many more questions we can ask ourselves about how we apply our communication skills. These you will find dealt with in other checklists – e.g. on **Counselling your staff** (page 158), **Managing meetings** (page 218), **Writing** (page 201), **Speaking in public** (page 226), and so on.

KEY IDEA

Communication is not just giving people information. It also involves responding to the information they give you.

Reading

Most managers feel they have too much to read. Typed and printed materials flow on to one's desk in a near-continuous stream. Our computer screens and even mobile phones present us with yet more text to deal with. Half of all this material is probably not worth reading; but how, without actually reading it, is one to know which half? And even the mainly worthless half may contain some information that is extremely helpful, if not absolutely essential, to one's effectiveness as a manager. So how does one sort the chaff from the grain and keep on top of one's reading?

Some managers try to give their closest attention to every piece of material that comes near them. This can leave them with little time for managing. Then someone suggests they take a speed-reading course. This puts them in a position to echo Woody Allen's testimonial 'Yes, I've just taken a speed-reading course. Very useful. I read *War and Peace* last night – all 1,400 pages. Took me 20 minutes. It's about Russia, isn't it?'

The quickest way to deal with your reading material is not to use speed-reading techniques, but to cut down on the amount you need to read. Efficient reading means being selective about what you read, and then reading it at whatever speed is most appropriate to the nature of the material and your purpose in reading it. There are three chief elements in reading efficiently:

- identify the purpose for which you are reading;
- have a system for handling reading materials;
- learn and apply appropriate reading techniques.

The following checklists should help.

What and why do you read?

Which of the following sorts of materials do you regularly expect to have to read?

- Letters ❑
- Memos or reports ❑
- Internet, e-mail or mobile phone text ❑
- Copies of letters, memos or reports sent to other people ❑
- Agendas and papers for future meetings ❑
- Minutes or notes of past meetings ❑
- Advertising/promotional circulars ❑
- Newspapers ❑
- Trade or professional journals ❑
- Selected articles or papers ❑
- Books (management or technical) ❑
- Others _____

_____

Now consider *why* you need to read them. Here we can pick out four chief purposes.

1 *Action* – where you need to do something in the foreseeable future as a result of your understanding of the materials.

2 *Internal information* – where the material may provide useful background information about what is going on within your organization.

3 *External information* – background information about what is happening in your field outside your organization.

4 *Professional learning* – where the material can be expected to contribute to your continuing learning and development as a manager or technical expert.

Alongside each of the items you picked out in the list above, write the most likely purpose (**1–4**) you would have in reading it.

Managing your reading materials

It helps to have a *system* for handling the materials you may be expected to read. Which of the following tips might you usefully be able to adopt?

- Get my name taken off the circulation list of publications that I never find relevant. ❑

- Ask people to stop sending me reports or copies of memos and e-mails that never concern me. ❑

- Ask team members to restrict their memos and routine reports to one side of A4 – and to keep e-mails even briefer. ❑

- Avoid creating unnecessary paperwork and screen-reading myself. ❑

- Ask one of my team to categorize materials for me under the four purposes set out above. ❑

- Ask one or more of my team to read certain materials for me and provide summaries. ❑

- Agree with fellow managers to share out the reading of professional and technical materials and tell each other the highlights once a month. ❑

- Guarantee myself a total of at least one hour a week reading materials that will contribute to my professional development. ❑

- Don't handle any material more than twice – once to decide what to do with it and once to do it. ❑

- Learn to be ruthless in saying 'no' to materials that don't deserve my attention. ❑

- If I decide not to do anything with some material, get rid of it straight away – into the waste paper bin or on to a colleague. ❑

- Create a logical filing system so that I know where to look for materials on different subjects or of different types or degrees of urgency. ❑

- Remember to inform my team of anything I've read that
  may interest or help them.   ❏

- Others _____

  _____

Towards a reading strategy

When faced with a pile of reading materials – whether physical or on a computer screen – some people start gamely at page 1 of the first item they come to and plough on, word by word, until they finish the last page of the item at the bottom of the pile. This is an inefficient way for a manager to work. The first essential of efficient reading is to be *selective*. This is a three-stage process.

1 Scan through the pile, glancing over every item, and throw out, delete or pass on any material that does not concern you.

2 With each item that does appear to be relevant, skim through it to get a general idea of what it is about – and discard it if it is unworthy of your closer attention.

3 Read carefully any item (or sections *within* an item) that survive this far. (If the material is lengthy and reaches you on a computer screen, you may prefer to print it out for easier reading.)

Skimming

The purpose of skimming (stage **2** above) is to get a feel for what (if anything) you might be expected to get out of the material and/or do about it. In doing so, one might ask oneself questions like those that follow. Which of them might be appropriate to the kinds of reading material you are faced with?

- Has this been sent exclusively to me?
- Who sent it?
- Do I have to do something about it?

- What is it about?
- With a journal, does the contents list help me decide which articles to consider further?
- With a book, does the contents page and/or the index help me to identify sections that might be worth closer study or to track down information I am looking for?
- With all materials:
  - what do the sub-headings (if any) tell me?
  - what can I pick up from a glance at any illustrations, lists, calculations, etc.?
  - can I get any clues from introductions, prefaces, etc.?
  - are there any useful summaries?
- If not, are the main points mentioned in the first or final paragraphs:
  - glancing through the paragraphs, do any key words leap out at me?
  - do I have any feelings about the author's main ideas, intentions or approach?
- For what purpose might I read this material (or parts of it) more carefully?
- What *questions* might I be looking to answer from any more careful reading?

Reading carefully

If some material appears to be worth reading carefully – e.g. for action or for learning – ask yourself questions like these.

- What is my purpose in reading this so carefully?
- What questions have been suggested by my earlier skimming?
- What are the main ideas? (The main idea of each paragraph is usually in the first or last sentence.)
- What evidence, examples, explanations and other detail are used to support or qualify each main idea?
- Are any main ideas or important details contained in diagrams, tables, photographs, etc?

- Which of the main ideas or important details are worth making a written note of?
- What is my assessment as I read the text? For example:
  - are its facts correct and up-to-date?
  - does it distinguish between fact and opinion?
  - are its examples, evidence, explanations, etc. plausible?
  - are its conclusions (main ideas) properly supported by evidence and examples?
  - would other conclusions follow equally well from the evidence offered?
  - how closely do the conclusions tie in with my experience?
  - is the author overlooking any aspects that seem important to me?
  - how might I use the ideas presented here?
  - is any of it worth reading again (now or later on)?
- What might I (or must I) *do* as a result of reading the text?
- Shall I write a summary of the material? (If so, why?)
- Is the text and/or my summary worth storing?
- Shall I discuss the material with anyone? (Who? Why? When?)
- What have I learned that is, or might be, of value to me?
- If the answer is 'nothing', how can I avoid wasting time on careful reading of such material again?
- Do I find myself continually backtracking to re-read earlier words in a sentence or paragraph? (Unless the material is very difficult to understand, try to keep your eyes moving downwards, if necessary by moving your finger down the page.)
- Am I frequently held up by not knowing the meaning of ordinary non-technical words? (If so look them up in a dictionary and write them down to enlarge your vocabulary.)
- Do I consciously try to read as fast as I can, bearing in mind the nature of the material and my purpose in reading it? (When skimming easy material you may manage to deal with 400–500 words per minute or more. When carefully reading more difficult material you may need to slow down to 100 words per minute or less.)

Writing

As a manager, you may need to spend quite a lot of time drafting letters, memos, reports and other printed or on-screen documents. You may be writing for your manager, for members of your team, for other people in your organization or for people outside the organization.

You will need to convey information, instructions, questions, decisions and suggestions in writing to people who, we hope, will read your words, understand what you mean by them and take the kind of action you would wish as a result. In order to bring this about, your writing will need to be readable, accurate and to the point.

Different people have different problems in producing such writing. Here are some of them (and I leave you to decide which are ever problems for you).

- deciding what is most worth saying;
- getting started;
- avoiding wordiness;
- keeping to the point;
- grammar;
- punctuation;
- vocabulary;
- spelling;
- style and readability.

The following checklists touch on all such problems, besides several others. You may also find it helpful to look at the checklists on **Communicating** (page 186).

What must you write?

Which of the following do you have to write?

- Letters and/or replies to other people's letters ❑
- Memos and/or replies to other people's memos ❑
- E-mail messages and replies to other people's messages ❑
- Reports or discussion documents ❑
- Comments on other people's reports, etc. ❑
- Minutes or notes of meetings ❑
- Articles for house journals, newsletters, etc. ❑
- Articles for trade or professional journals ❑
- Advertising or promotional material ❑
- Others _____

'Quick and dirty' approaches to writing

Certain writing tasks simply do not deserve the full power of your creative energies. Consider whether any of the following approaches might suffice for some of your work.

- Delegate the writing of routine items or replies to a properly-briefed secretary or assistant ❑
- Use standard letters (or standard paragraphs to be chosen from and/or amended) for routine correspondence ❑
- If your reply can be brief, write it on the incoming memo or letter, send a photocopy to the sender, and put the original in your files ❑
- If there is no room on the original, even for a brief response, write your comments on an adhesive-edged 'speed memo' and stick that on instead ❑

- If the incoming letter has an e-mail address on it, and needs only an acknowledgement or brief reply, consider replying by e-mail ❑

- Don't write if a phone call will save time (and be realistic about how many of your organization's 'person-minutes' would be consumed by a written item) ❑

- Don't write if a phone call would be better – if you need to exchange ideas or negotiate ❑

- Don't write or phone if you need to see the other person face-to-face while you talk ❑

- Persuade your manager or fellow managers that you can be relied upon to report exceptions – rather than having to give regular blow-by-blow accounts of how things are running quite according to plan ❑

Writing plainly and effectively

The best one-sentence guide to effective writing is: *Write as you talk*. Put down on paper or on screen what you might say to the reader if he or she were there in front of you. Which of the following guidelines can you follow in the kind of writing you have to do?

Write conversationally

- Use personal pronouns ('I', 'you', 'we').

- Use contractions ('I'll', 'we've', 'mustn't') where you'd use them in speech.

- Use rhetorical questions – questions you pose at the beginning of a paragraph and then go on to answer yourself.

- Be friendly, informal and light of touch without being matey, slangy or chatty.

Choose your words carefully

- Don't use several words where one will do – e.g. not 'in the great majority of cases' but 'usually'.

- Use familiar, everyday words – e.g. not 'relinquish', 'terminate' and 'exacerbate', but 'give up', 'end', and 'worsen'.

- Avoid long-winded phrases and official-sounding gobbledegook – e.g. not 'They exhibited economy in the deployment of veracity', but 'They lied'.

- Use precise words rather than general, abstract ones – e.g. not 'Extreme danger is associated with the incorrect operation of this equipment', but 'Keep the safety shield down or this machine may kill you'.

- Use active not passive verbs – e.g. not 'A trial was carried out', but 'We (or whoever it was) carried out a trial'.

- Use specialist terms only if you can be sure your readers are already familiar with them, or if you define them in what you are writing.

If spelling causes you problems

- Use the spellchecker on your computer.
- Keep a dictionary at hand.
- Make a list of words that give you trouble.
- Break each word into its separate syl-la-bles and underline the syl-la-<u>ble</u> that gives you trouble.
- Write out each word correctly several times.
- Practise seeing such spellings in your mind's eye.
- Learn what few spelling rules are at all helpful – e.g. 'i before e except after c (but only when the sound is ee)', and 'single consonant after a long vowel (as in robing) but double consonant if the vowel is short (as in robbing)'.
- Keep using your dictionary.

Simplify your sentences

- Keep your sentences short (rarely more than 20 words). Short sentences will:
  - help you avoid grammatical errors;
  - help you spot them more easily if you do make them;
  - save you from many punctuation problems.

- Avoid writing sentences which, like this one, having phrases and clauses sprouting within them – each with their own qualifications (some more, and some less, to the point than others) to make, are not only too long but also too complex for easy reading, and are better split into several shorter ones.

Keep your paragraphs short

- Start each paragraph with your 'topic sentence' which carries the main idea.
- Lead up to the main idea as your final sentence.
- Use the rest of the paragraph to elaborate on the main idea or else lead up to it.
- If you write a paragraph and see that it contains more than one main idea, make each the topic of a separate paragraph.

Punctuate for meaning

- Write short sentences and you will have much less trouble with punctuation.
- Use punctuation to substitute for the pauses and emphases you would use if you were speaking to your reader.
- If you have trouble imagining this, try reading your sentences aloud.
- If you want your reader to pause only briefly, insert a comma.
- A full stop gives a longer pause.
- If you want to make a comment (not too lengthy) on what you have just written, enclose it in brackets.
- Alternatively – perhaps to make your writing more open in texture – set off the comment with a pair of dashes.
- If you want two short sentences to be linked together use a semi-colon; this gives a pause longer than a comma but shorter than a full stop.
- If you want to give particular emphasis to a word, <u>underline</u> it or have it printed **bold** or in CAPITALS.
- If you must emphasize a complete statement use the exclamation mark! (But one only!!! and not too often!)

- Use 'bullets'/numbers/letters as punctuation marks to tell the reader you are presenting a list of related items.

Measure your readability

(a) Count how many sentences you have written.

(b) Count the number of words with three or more syllables.

(c) Divide (b) by (a) to find the average number of long words per sentence.

If this average (call it your complexity quotient, or CQ) exceeds 3, your writing will be more difficult to read than that of most novelists. Try this test on some material that you know your readers do find readable, e.g. their favourite newspaper.

Layout and presentation

It's often not enough to have good ideas and express them well. If your document is to look attractive to readers, and enable them to grasp its structure and find their way around in it, it will also need to be well laid out. Here are some questions to ask yourself.

- Is it clear at a glance what the document is about (e.g. a title, or heading in a letter)? ❑
- Might readers find it helpful if I insert occasional headings or sub-headings? ❑
- Shall I distinguish between headings and sub-headings by using capitals and lower-case letters? ❑
- Are my paragraphs short enough? ❑
- Shall I number my paragraphs? ❑
- Will I sometimes get my points over more clearly in a list (like this one) rather than in a prose paragraph? ❑
- Will graphs, tables or diagrams sometimes be needed instead of, or as well as, prose? ❑
- Would it help to draw boxes around any items? ❑

- Do I need to emphasize any of the text by using
  underlining or CAPITALS? ❏

- Are my lines of type short enough for easy reading?
  (Lines with more than about 65 characters – letters or
  spaces – may be difficult to read.) ❏

- Is there enough space between lines? (The longer the
  line, the more space is needed between lines.) ❏

- Is there enough space around the margins of the text?
  (Don't let the pages look too dense with print.) ❏

- If the document is a lengthy one, does the reader, need:
  - a table of contents? ❏
  - one or more summaries? ❏
  - an index? ❏

- Can any of the content be put in an appendix for
  optional reading? ❏

- Should the document be presented in any special kind
  of folder or cover? ❏

Tackling the writing task

Many of the following hints and tips may be most applicable when writing lengthy pieces – longer memos or e-mails, reports, proposals, etc. But you may find that some are applicable to writing shorter documents like letters and brief memos. Alongside any of the following you think might be particularly helpful, jot down the kind of document you might use it for.

- Decide first why you are writing:
  - to give someone information they have asked for
  - to give them information you think they need (why?)
  - to request information yourself
  - to persuade someone to a point of view
  - to enable or encourage them to take action
  - to get them off your back

- Ask yourself what knowledge (or misinformation) and opinions (or prejudices) your reader may possess which you need to take into account in your writing

- If you haven't already got a deadline by which the writing must be finished, set yourself one

- Where feasible, let your potential readers know when to expect the material from you

- If the writing requires some preliminary research and thinking time, set yourself a deadline for starting the actual writing

- However brief the document, make sure it has a clear beginning, middle and end:
  - introduction (why you are writing)
  - middle (what you have to say)
  - conclusion (so what is the reader expected to think or do as a result of what you have said?)

- Jot down the main topics or points you want to mention in each section (and their sequence) before you begin writing sentences

- Don't feel you must write the document in the order in which it is to be read. If you find the beginning difficult, start somewhere else

- Get something written as soon as possible to 'prime the pump' – even knowing you may scrap it later

- As you write, keep in mind the reader(s) you are addressing and ask yourself, sentence by sentence, how they are likely to respond to your words

- Aim to 'brainstorm' your way through your first rough draft in one sitting, if at all possible

- If time allows, put your first draft aside for a day or two so you can look at it again with a fresh eye

	Yes	No
- Criticize your draft severely:		
– are my facts correct?	❏	❏
– are they complete enough?	❏	❏
– are they all relevant?	❏	❏

	Yes	No
– do my conclusions or recommendations follow logically from the facts?	❏	❏
– have I dealt with all likely objections?	❏	❏
– are my words and sentences short enough? (Do I have a CQ of 3 or less? – see page 206.)	❏	❏
– have I avoided mistakes in spelling, punctuation and grammar?	❏	❏
– does it read smoothly and easily?	❏	❏
– is it laid out (headings, spacing, etc.), so that readers can easily find their way into and around the material?	❏	❏
– can anything be cut out?	❏	❏

If you have time, and the document is important enough, get comments from someone (and/or sleep on it) before you send off a final draft. Don't miss your deadline trying to make the document perfect.

KEY IDEA

Whatever you write, read it aloud. Anything you find tedious or awkward to speak will be equally so for your readers to read.

Listening

Research has shown that managers spend perhaps 45 per cent of their time listening to people talk. But how much of that is just 'hearing' rather than true listening? If we are really listening, we are being active – we are doing something with what we are hearing. We are thinking about it. Our *minds* are working on it (not just our ears).

One of the troubles is that we can think far faster than the other person can talk. So it is easy to get distracted by thoughts of our own – especially thoughts about what we intend to say next. (How often do we see television interviewers asking a question to which they've just had the answer – because they were clearly too busy thinking about posing the next question to notice that their guest covered it while dealing with the *previous* question!)

Furthermore, much of what we have to listen to may strike us as unappealing. Managers have to deal with lies, excuses, complaints, accusations and expressions of despair. There will be people who seem determined to waste your time, bore you to death, sell you something you don't want, persuade you out of your better judgement or push you around. No wonder there's sometimes a temptation to 'tune out'.

An effective manager is one who knows how to listen – and listen *actively* – whatever the circumstances. This means concentrating on what is being said, and on the way it is being said. An active listener is looking for *meaning* in what he or she is hearing. Could you, at the very least, express in your own words what the other person has conveyed to you – to *their* satisfaction?

The experience of being actively listened to may be quite novel to many speakers. Certainly it will make many people feel more appreciated and taken note of. It may even transform the way some people see themselves and feel about themselves. This outcome of active listening may be very much to be desired in counselling your staff, for instance. But active listening is important for the manager in all kinds of situations, from job interviewing or negotiating with a supplier to holding their own in a meeting. The checklists in this section are relevant to many of the other sections of this book. (You may also find it useful to look at the checklists on **Communicating**, page 186.)

To whom must you listen?

First of all, consider the number and variety of people you may need to listen to. Tick whichever of the following have expected you to listen to them during the last working week.

- Your manager ❏
- Your manager's manager ❏
- Fellow managers in your organization ❏
- Consultants or advisors (internal or external) ❏
- Your team members ❏
- Their staff (if any) ❏

- Other managers' team members   ❑
- Union representatives   ❑
- Job applicants   ❑
- Customers or clients   ❑
- Suppliers   ❑
- Competitors   ❑
- Professional acquaintances in other organizations   ❑
- Press, radio or TV representatives   ❑
- Others _____

Sometimes you listen chiefly because you need to hear what the other person has to say, sometimes because the other person needs to be listened to. Tick the following 'listening purposes' according to whether they are chiefly for your benefit, chiefly for theirs, or whether they benefit both.

	You	Them	Both
To obtain information	❑	❑	❑
To learn people's opinions	❑	❑	❑
To explore their feelings and attitudes	❑	❑	❑
To clarify a misunderstanding	❑	❑	❑
To assess or appraise the person	❑	❑	❑
To help them talk through a problem	❑	❑	❑
To encourage their creativity	❑	❑	❑
To make them feel appreciated	❑	❑	❑
To ensure that they also listen to you	❑	❑	❑

- Others _____

Clearly there are many people to listen to and many reasons why you may be doing so – both yours and theirs.

How well do you listen?

Most of us have our weaknesses as listeners, though few of us are aware of them. Which of the following weaknesses do you recognize in yourself?

Selective listening

	Yes	No
• Are there some individuals you avoid having to listen to?	❏	❏
• Are there certain *categories* of people you find difficult to listen to?	❏	❏
• Would someone's appearance prejudice you so that you could not listen objectively?	❏	❏
• Might a person's accent or way of speaking make him/her scarcely worth listening to?	❏	❏
• Do you 'tune out' on certain topics?	❏	❏
• Do you refuse to listen to things that may make you feel uncomfortable?	❏	❏
• Do you pay attention only to the good things (or only to the bad things) you hear?	❏	❏
• Do you listen chiefly for facts and overlook expressions of feeling, opinion or prejudice?	❏	❏
• Do you listen purely for your own purposes without thinking what the other person needs?	❏	❏

Attention

	Yes	No
• Do you let your mind wander or pursue thoughts of your own?	❏	❏
• Do you spend most of the time thinking what *you* are going to say next?	❏	❏
• Are you easily distracted by other things going on around you?	❏	❏

	Yes	No
● Do you have ways of kidding the speaker you are paying attention when you are not?	❏	❏
● Does your body language (wandering gaze, stifled yawn, tapping foot or drumming fingers) ever reveal that you are getting bored, impatient or irritable?	❏	❏

Interruptions

	Yes	No
● Are you always itching to jump in with your own ideas as soon as the other person pauses?	❏	❏
● If the other person says something you disagree with do you interrupt to put your point of view?	❏	❏
● If you can guess the end of a person's sentence, do you complete it for him/her?	❏	❏
● If so, do you then continue talking yourself?	❏	❏
● Do you try to stop the speaker if you feel he or she is getting angry or upset?	❏	❏

Which of the above is your one *worst* listening weakness? Circle the box to remind you, and consciously try to overcome that weakness during your next week of listening to people.

Giving feedback

To be an active listener you need to give appropriate feedback to the person who is talking. That is you need to *let them know* that you are paying attention and trying to understand things from their point of view. Which of the following might be appropriate in any of the kinds of listening *you* need to do?

● Reflecting back what the other person seems to be saying by restating it in my own words	❏
● Telling the other person what feeling or attitude I seem to hear them expressing	❏

- Inviting them to comment on my understanding ❏
- Asking them to say more about things I don't understand ❏
- Happily tolerating pauses, which may encourage the talker to carry on and dig deeper ❏
- Asking open-ended questions (e.g. 'Why', 'What', 'How'?) that leave the talker free to say what they want ❏
- Ensuring that my contributions are no lengthier than they need be ❏
- Expressing:
  - approval ❏
  - disapproval ❏
  - both approval and disapproval ❏
  - neither approval nor disapproval ❏
- Offering diagnoses or solutions of my own ❏
- Refusing to offer my own diagnoses or solutions ❏
- Using non-verbal noises (*Mmm* and *Uh-huh*) ❏
- Using body language – e.g. eye contact, nods, facial expressions, different body postures ❏
- Responding to *their* non-verbal noises or body language (especially if they seem anxious or angry) by encouraging or calming them ❏
- Summarizing all the key points I believe the other person has made ❏
- Remembering what they have said (even if I have to make notes afterwards) ❏
- Showing by what I say or do later that I have remembered what the person told me ❏
- Others _____

Clearly, different situations (counselling, job interviewing, staff coun-selling, customer complaints, meetings, etc.) will call for different kinds of active listening. I leave you to decide which of the above approaches may be useful for the different kinds of listening you regularly need to do.

> **KEY IDEA**
>
> If you regularly listen actively to other people you may find they repay the compliment by listening that way to you.

Telephoning

The telephone is an invaluable management tool if used properly, but it can easily make us its slaves. Do you sprint along the corridor to dive into your office because you've heard your phone ringing?Is your mobile always switched on? Do you interrupt your discussion with someone who has made an appointment to come to see you, in order to respond for minutes on end to someone else who just decided to ring you up? Do you yourself get on the phone the minute a need occurs to you, rather than considering whether a phone call is the best way of dealing with the matter, and whether now is the best time for it anyway? If so, you are not alone.

But we *can* be more ruthless and systematic about the way we use the telephone – rather than letting it use us. As a result we can save time, and work more efficiently. The following checklists contain some hints and tips that may help in this.

Making calls

- Don't pick up the phone the minute the thought of telephoning someone occurs to you. First ask:
  - is this matter best dealt with by telephoning (rather than face to face or in writing)?
  - if I shall have to put it in writing or meet the other person about it anyway, is phoning a waste of time?
  - am I likely to get drawn into time-wasting discussions of other matters besides what I want to talk about?

- even if the call is worth making, do I really need to make it at this moment (rather than in my daily 'telephone period')?

- Timetable a regular half-hour or so each day in which you will try to make all your telephone calls.

- Get all the necessary paperwork to hand before making your calls.

- Have additional reading material that you can be checking or skimreading in any necessary gaps between or within calls.

- If possible, get a secretary or assistant to make your calls and put them through only when they have made contact.

- Be quite clear why you are making the call. Are you:
  - giving information?
  - asking for information?
  - requesting action?
  - or what?

- What kind of response are you wanting from the other person?

- If there are several points you want to raise, make a list of them before you call.

- Decide on the maximum time you will hold the line waiting for the person you want to talk with.

- Unless you think they'll be unobtainable later, say you'll ring back and get on with the next call.

- If the person you want is out, ask whether there is anyone else who might be able to deal with your call.

- In case you are greeted by an answering machine, or by someone who cannot help, have a precise message ready for them to pass on:
  - your full name;
  - your organization;
  - your telephone number;
  - the subject of your call;
  - the kind of response you are expecting.

- Make a point of telephoning to check the date, time, place (and necessity) of distant meetings before you start your journey.

Receiving calls

- Let regular callers know when is the best time of day to telephone you.
- Also let them know the times to avoid.
- Consider asking unexpected callers to ring back in your 'telephone period' (or whenever it best suits you).
- If possible, brief a secretary or assistant to intercept and screen your incoming calls. For example, are there:
  - people you are just not available to?
  - people you want referred elsewhere?
  - people who should be asked to call back at a specified time?
  - people you will call back at a specified time?
  - people you are willing to talk to whenever they call?
- If someone else is putting calls through to you, make sure they don't do so until the actual person who wants to speak to you (not their assistant) is on the line.
- If you can't get human help, set up voice mail or other answering technology to ask callers to leave a message and/or ring back at a certain time.
- If you simply cannot afford to be interrupted and have no one to intercept incoming calls, take the phone off the hook or unplug it, or hide out in a room where calls won't reach you.

Managing telephone conversations

- Don't let business calls drift into prolonged social or general chit-chat.
- Have a few standard ways of politely bringing a conversation to a close – e.g. 'My manager has just called for me', or 'I'm due in a meeting upstairs', etc.
- Consider having a timer ticking away by your phone while you talk.
- Make sure that you or the other person sums up the conversation so that both of you can agree what has been said – especially if one or both have agreed to take some action.

- Consider making notes.

- Confirm in writing any important matter that has been agreed – especially if you fear the other person might forget, or wish to deny it.

- Consider keeping a log of each of your telephone calls for a week:
  - who called whom?
  - when?
  - purpose?
  - how long?
  - how much undue chit-chat?
  - outcome worthwhile?
  - written or face-to-face follow-up needed?
  - how much of an interruption to higher-priority work?
  - any other problems?

KEY IDEA

Don't let people waste your precious time with their telephone calls – and be equally careful not to make calls that waste theirs.

Managing meetings

Meetings come in for a lot of criticism in organizations. There are too many of them. They're a waste of precious productive time. They're very expensive in salary costs, travel, etc. They provide too much of a personality platform for windbags. They slow down decision-making and discourage individual enterprise. They concentrate on trivialities and gloss over the real issues. And so on.

At the same time, much of an organization's business could not be done without meetings. They can enable us to share experience and obtain information from one another. They can ensure that people with opposing viewpoints have the satisfaction of arguing their cases in public. They can contribute to team-building and better co-ordination of effort. They can produce better ideas and solutions than could be produced by individuals working separately. And so on.

Clearly there are many reasons why a meeting may flounder – it may, for instance, be unnecessary, or be held at the wrong time, or be poorly controlled. But the plain fact is that meetings are unavoidable. So how can we avoid the pitfalls and reap all the potential benefits? The answer is that we need to *manage* them. And this applies whether we are chairing a meeting or 'merely' participating in it. The following checklists are concerned with four main aspects:

- Evaluating a meeting.
- Setting up a meeting.
- Chairing a meeting.
- Participating in a meeting.

Evaluating a meeting

Meetings can go wrong in several ways. Think about the last meeting you attended. Consider which of the following criticisms would apply.

- The purpose of the meeting was unclear ❑
- A meeting was unnecessary to achieve the purpose ❑
- Some of the members had no reason to be there ❑
- Not all members knew who all the other members were ❑
- Some people who should have been there were not ❑
- The meeting suffered from lack of leadership ❑
- No one was taking adequate notes or minutes ❑
- The meeting was disrupted by, for example:
  - members arriving late ❑
  - members leaving early ❑
  - members slipping in and out ❑
  - members going off to get information ❑
  - members dealing with visitors or phone calls ❑
  - members quarrelling ❑
- Some people were allowed to do more talking than their ideas justified ❑

- People with important things to say were not given a proper hearing ❏
- Some people were allowed to grind their own axes and score points rather than address the real topics ❏
- The person in the chair talked too much ❏
- The chair seemed unwilling to discuss viewpoints contrary to his or her own ❏
- Important topics were discussed without notice having been given before the meeting ❏
- Too much time was spent on some topics and too little on others ❏
- Discussion was allowed to ramble on after decisions had been reached ❏
- The meeting ran out of time ❏
- The meeting was allowed to go on long beyond the agreed finishing time ❏
- Several topics failed to result in decisions ❏
- Decisions were taken on inadequate evidence ❏
- Members disagreed as to what decisions had been reached ❏
- Members felt their time was wasted ❏
- The costs (salaries, expenses, etc.) involved in having the meeting were not justified by the results ❏
- Others _____

Some such checklist is worth applying to every meeting you attend – *especially* if you were in the chair.

If you're thinking of calling a meeting

First ask yourself some questions.

	Yes	No

- Are there any clear and important purposes for having a meeting? (Don't call a meeting just because you always have one on Friday mornings – not if there's nothing that needs discussing.) ❏ ❏

- Which of these purposes might your meeting have:
  - sharing experience? ❏
  - keeping myself informed? ❏
  - informing other people? ❏
  - training? ❏
  - brainstorming for new ideas? ❏
  - solving problems? ❏
  - evaluating proposals? ❏
  - making decisions? ❏
  - airing grievances? ❏
  - obtaining advice? ❏
  - giving other people advice? ❏
  - promoting team spirit? ❏
  - providing a target/deadline? ❏
  - consulting vested interests? ❏
  - others _____

  _____

- Do I know which of the above is the most important purpose? ❏ ❏

- Could we hold the 'meeting' without getting together face to face, e.g. by video conferencing, telephone conferencing, computer conferencing or e-mail? ❏ ❏

If you are chairing the meeting

If you are chairing the meeting, its success or otherwise will be very much in your hands. Before the meeting you will need to:

1 answer the four questions in the checklist above;

2 read all the background papers;

3 consider how members of the meeting are likely to respond;

4 decide how you might need to handle them in order to get the most appropriate outcomes from the meeting.

Then, at the meeting itself make sure that the following happen.

- Start the meeting on time and don't smile indulgently at late-comers ❑
- Be cheerful and friendly and put people at their ease ❑
- But be brisk and business-like, making clear that you are in charge ❑
- Remind members of the outcomes of the previous meeting if there was one and/or review the minutes ❑
- Explain the purpose of the present meeting ❑
- Mention the main items on the agenda ❑
- Tell the group when the meeting will finish and point out how much discussion time there is for each item ❑
- Control the discussion:
  - invite contributions from the people most capable of advancing each topic – usually those you briefed before the meeting ❑
  - invite contributions from other members, taking care that no one is allowed to hog the debate ❑
  - do not hog the discussion yourself but do make comments or ask questions where appropriate ❑
  - listen with great concentration but also observe how other people are reacting to what is being said ❑
  - be firm but friendly in reining back the discussion if people start drifting from the point at issue ❑
  - encourage people who have not spoken to do so if they wish ❑
  - ensure that all disagreements are made public and discussed rather than taken away to fester ❑

- but step in decisively (without losing your own temper) if people begin quarrelling ❏
- remind people of the passing time and keep pressing them towards a conclusion (if one looks attainable) ❏
- where appropriate (and especially after each item on the agenda) summarize the discussion so far and any conclusions/decisions that have been reached ❏
- ask the group for their confirmation or amendments ❏
- press on to the next item on the agenda ❏
- if some discussion item must take longer than you allowed, decide whether to extend the meeting or to leave some items for another meeting ❏

● At the end of the meeting, summarize what has been achieved and thank the people present ❏

● Remind people of who has agreed to do what by when ❏

● Agree the date, time, place and purpose of the next meeting if there is to be one ❏

● Finish the meeting on time ❏

● Arrange for minutes or notes to be circulated summarizing the main points agreed and who is to do what ❏

● Consider whether a statement about the meeting needs to be made available to people who did not attend ❏

● Take whatever action you need to take in view of the discussion at the meeting ❏

If you are a member of a meeting

Here are some guidelines worth thinking about when you are attending meetings called or chaired by someone else.

● Decide whether you really need attend. (Might it be better for another member of your team to go instead?) ❏

- Decide your purpose(s) in attending the meeting, for example:
  - to give information ❑
  - to obtain information ❑
  - to safeguard your group's interests ❑
  - to present a proposal ❑
  - to question someone else's proposal ❑
  - to solve problems ❑
  - to make decisions ❑
  - to create new ideas ❑
  - others _____

(See also the list of purposes on page 221.)

- Decide whether there are any items you wish to see put on the agenda ❑

- Read and think about the agenda and/or discussion papers ❑

- If you are to present a report or proposal, prepare it in good time and see that any necessary papers for discussion are circulated ❑

- If you have any doubts about the acceptability of your report or proposal, sound out influential members of the meeting in order to rally support and decide how best to present your case ❑

- Consider how you will handle the kinds of objections you may get ❑

- Arrive at the meeting on time ❑

- If there is no agenda and/or no obvious purpose for the meeting, ask what the purpose is ❑

- Ask about the purpose again later if the discussion strikes you as aimless ❑

- If no one is in the chair, consider whether you want to volunteer for the role ❑

- If no one has the role of record-keeper – a role that can give the holder almost as much power as the chair to focus and summarize the discussion – consider volunteering for it ❏

- If you think it important to make your mark on the meeting, especially with people you have not met with before, speak early and make your presence felt throughout the meeting (without seeming to hog it) ❏

- Concentrate hard on what is going on and make sure that what you have to say is relevant and worth hearing and has not been said already ❏

- If the topic is unfamiliar to you, don't make statements or ask questions until you have heard what your more expert colleagues have had to say about it ❏

- If you have nothing to say, keep quiet but show that you are actively listening (and perhaps taking notes) ❏

- If speaking, make your points clearly and succinctly – don't ramble ❏

- Take into account the effect your remarks are having on other members ❏

- If you have a report or proposal to present, concentrate on the main points and/or benefits (don't assume everyone will have read and fully understood any papers you circulated previously) ❏

- Be open to incorporating other people's ideas into your proposal – aim for it to be seen as 'ours' rather than 'mine' ❏

- Try to meet all objections with counter-arguments (and patient good humour) ❏

- If it looks as if your proposal is going to be rejected, try to get the decision delayed (so that you can do more work on it, and on the objectors) ❏

- If it is rejected, accept defeat gracefully ❏

- In questioning or criticizing other people's proposals, be as courteous as you would wish them to be to you ❏

- Don't leave the meeting without being sure what you are expected to do as a result of it, and what other people are expected to do that might affect you ❏

- Ask yourself what you have learned about the other people that may help you in your future dealings with them ❏

- Ask yourself whether you have achieved your purpose(s) in the meeting – and if not, why not? ❏

KEY IDEA

Don't blame other people if meetings seem a waste of time. If you've got to attend them, make sure you get something useful out of them.

Speaking in public

A manager's job usually involves some public speaking. Every so often, you may need to get on your feet in front of an audience and give a more or less formal talk or presentation. You may be talking to your own team, but more likely you will be talking to other managers, to people from elsewhere in the organization, or maybe to people from outside. Your effectiveness as a public speaker may turn out to be a major factor in how your career progresses.

Some managers seem to revel in public speaking; others dread it. Many are nervous about it in advance, but nevertheless come across splendidly when the moment arrives. The one-time British Prime Minister Harold Macmillan, for instance, was regarded as one of the outstanding orators of his time, but he later admitted to being physically sick for days before he had to make any major speech in Parliament.

Would you be nervous at the prospect of speaking in public? If not, you ought to be. Without a certain amount of nervousness, your adrenalin would not flow and you would appear dull, lifeless, bored and boring. Too much nervousness, on the other hand, could spoil your performance, so it needs to be controlled. The following checklists should help you to develop a well-justified self-confidence, for they deal with the four chief components to speaking effectively in public:

- Controlling nervousness.
- Considering your audience.
- Preparing your talk.
- Delivering your talk.

Whatever you feel about it, public speaking is another essential management skill. As long as you don't fall back on that time-worn excuse: 'Unaccustomed as I am to public speaking . . .', as long as you are prepared to *get* accustomed – with as much practice as necessary, the skill is one you can get better and better at.

Controlling nervousness

Would you admit to yourself that you might be nervous about any of the following? Which one would worry you most?

- Not knowing what people expect of me   ❑
- Fearing that I have nothing to say worth hearing   ❑
- Uncertainty about why I am speaking   ❑
- Not comparing well with other speakers I have heard   ❑
- Giving a muddled or boring talk   ❑
- Anxiety about having to use 'visual aids'   ❑
- Fearing that I will 'dry up'   ❑
- Not having a 'public platform' type of voice   ❑
- Having to deal with audience reactions   ❑
- Being rejected by the audience   ❑
- Others _____

The key to controlling any such nervousness lies in:

- Considering your audience.
- Preparing your talk.

This is what the next two checklists are about.

Considering your audience

Here are the kinds of questions to ask yourself right at the start.

- Who will be in my audience?
- How many of them will there be?
- Do I know any of them already?
- What might they be expecting to hear from me?
- How might they use what they hear?
- Will they assume I am qualified to speak on the subject?
- Can I assume they are reasonably well-disposed towards me?
- Am I aiming to inform them or persuade them?
- Will it be clear why the subject should matter to them?
- How much will some of them know about it already?
- How little will some of them know about it?
- Will any of them have misconceptions about it?
- Will any have strong feelings about it?
- Will any have beliefs different from mine?
- Can I usefully discuss what might go into the talk with some likely members of the audience *before* I prepare it?
- Can I collect from them any points of interest I might usefully refer to or any relevant anecdotes I can quote?

N.B. Don't let yourself get drawn into speaking to this audience at all unless you believe that you can say something worth their hearing on the subject in question.

Preparing the talk

Make sure you give yourself as much time as possible for preparing your talk. And remember to make a note of ideas that occur to you while you are in the bath or walking your dog.

Thinking about the situation

- When is the talk to be given?
- Does this allow me enough preparation time?
- How long is the talk meant to last? (Don't be persuaded to talk for more than 40 minutes without interruption; 20–30 minutes may be more productive.)
- Will there/can there be discussion or questions during and/or after the talk?
- Will there be other speakers before and/or after me?
- If the audience is likely to be too big, can I split it up and give the talk more than once?
- Where will the talk take place?
- How will the audience be seated in relation to where I shall be speaking from?
- Will they have any problems seeing me or hearing me clearly?
- What audio-visual aids can be used?
- What about the acoustics, seating pattern, etc?
- Who will make any practical arrangements?
- Are all the above satisfactory for what I want to do (or can I fit in with them anyway)?

Purpose and content

- What is the main purpose of my talk – to inform, to persuade, to inspire, to train or what?
- What (if anything) do I want my audience to do as a result of my talk?
- What will be my overall message? (Try to sum it up in a single sentence, for example: 'We must innovate or perish'.)

- What are the main points I'll need to make in getting this message across? (Three main points are usually about the maximum an audience can be expected to take in.)
- Have I got all the information I need?
- Or do I need to consult books or other materials, or other people?
- What will be the title of my talk?

Structuring the talk

- What facts, examples and arguments will best get my main ideas across?
- Am I being careful to avoid trying to squeeze in everything I know on the subject?
- Shall I follow the old military instructor's advice: 'First I tell them what I'm going to tell them; then I tell them; then I tell them what I've told them.'?
- How else might I ensure that the talk has a clear beginning, middle and end?
- How can I get off to an interesting start? Consider:
  - showing how the subject relates to the interests or experience of the audience;
  - relating it to some local people, places or events;
  - reminiscing about how I got involved in the subject;
  - telling an *illuminating* anecdote or story;
  - comparing definitions of the key word in my title;
  - quoting other authorities on the subject;
  - asking some pertinent questions;
  - giving advance notice of my overall message and/or my (three?) main points;
  - telling the audience what I hope they may get from the talk.
- What will be the most logical flow of ideas for my main points in the middle of the talk?
- What supporting examples, evidence or arguments do I have to put across?

- Do I need to use linking phrases – to keep the audience aware of how each idea relates to what has gone before and what is coming after?

- Do I need to summarize from time to time?

- Does my knowledge of the audience help me choose the most appropriate form of words in which to express these ideas?

- How can I bring the talk to a satisfying conclusion? Shall I:
  - repeat my main points?
  - state my one-sentence 'overall message'?
  - pose the audience a provocative question?
  - call for some kind of action?

Methods

- Do I intend to give the audience a 'handout', e.g. summary in advance, or sample materials that I wish to refer to at some point?

- Do I intend to use any visual aids, e.g. a flip chart or an overhead projector?

- Shall I ask (or allow) the audience to offer examples, questions or comments at any point during the talk?

- Do I want to do so at the end?

- Shall I prime a few friends in the audience to ask any particular questions?

- In delivering the talk do I plan to:
  - read from a full script?
  - memorize a full script?
  - speak from detailed notes?
  - refer only to 'skeleton notes' (headings, sub-headings and key phrases)?
  - talk around a handout I give the audience?
  - talk around slides projected on a screen?

- If I feel I must read the talk, how can I make it as *conversational* as possible? For example, by using:
  - short sentences?
  - simple sentence structure?
  - everyday words (not long-winded phrases)?

  - only jargon that will be familiar to my audience?
  - conversational turns of phrase?
  - first person pronouns ('I', 'we', 'you', etc.)?
  - lightness of touch?

- If my material is written out in full, how can I make it as legible as possible? For example, by having it:
  - typed?
  - in a large typeface?
  - double-spaced?
  - with prominent headings?
  - on one side only?
  - on A4 sheets of paper?

- Or do I feel confident enough, having written the talk in full, to summarize it as a series of headings and key phrases on numbered cards or sheets of paper?

- Can I *rehearse* the talk by trying it out on friends, spouse, colleagues or self, and make whatever improvements seem necessary after I have heard how it sounds?

- Having rehearsed, would I now feel confident about speaking from skeleton notes, a handout or slides as mentioned above?

Delivering the talk

Having prepared thoroughly, you will not fail. But the extent to which you succeed depends also on what you do on the day. Before you even begin, check the following.

- All your notes, handouts, visual aids, etc. are ready for use.
- Any necessary equipment such as a microphone is working properly and heating, seating, lighting and ventilation are as you require.
- Chat informally with one or two members of your audience if you can.

When you are satisfied that everything, including you and the audience, is ready, here are some checklists to work through.

Aim for a good first impression

- Wait until everyone is quiet.
- Start with energy and enthusiasm.
- Look members of your audience in the eyes.
- Make your introductory remarks without having to refer to your notes.
- Stand still and upright – and don't wave your hands about.
- Smile a little and look relaxed, confident and in command.
- Make sure that your voice gets to the back of the room.

Speak conversationally.

- Imagine you are talking to people you know reasonably well (even if you are not).
- Speak distinctly and not too fast.
- Use natural pauses and emphases.
- Look at each individual in turn while you talk.
- Don't preach or talk down to your audience
- Be light of touch and good humoured.
- But don't bring in jokes unless they are truly relevant (and funny).
- Be yourself.

Keep your grip on the audience

- Maintain eye contact with your audience.
- Don't bury your head in your notes. (Lift them up instead.)
- If you must read from a script, look up as often as you can.
- Watch out for signs of puzzlement or restlessness.
- Respond to any such signs you see.
- Don't accept questions in mid-talk unless you really want to.
- If you get a question that is difficult to answer:
  - say, without embarrassment, that you can't answer that one; or
  - say you'll discuss it with the questioner afterwards; or
  - invite the audience to offer answers; or
  - answer a slightly different question; or

      – ask a counter-question of the questioner (e.g. ask him/ her to spell out what lies behind the question).

- Avoid distractions – overgesturing or pacing about.
- Don't 'er' and 'um' – better to have a moment's silence.
- Watch the time!

Finish conclusively

- Let your audience know the end is in sight.
- Have the exact wording of your final sentence clearly in mind.
- Finish off as vigorously as you began.

KEY IDEA

Never, ever, apologize to your audience for lack of speaking ability.

Managing with IT

Computers provide us with a means of creating and shifting information at speeds and in quantities that would have been unthinkable 20 years ago. But this facility comes at a price. Not so much the cost of the equipment and software (which is constantly falling in terms of what you get for your money). The chief costs for the manager are the time and effort involved in:

- keeping up to date with what is newly available;
- assessing how far it is worth using and;
- learning how to use it.

New technology often presents us with a heavy learning curve. This can make us want to be pretty sure about a new medium before we decide it's worth learning how to use. (And some managers always suspect that an even more useful medium will appear on the scene before they've finished learning about the current one!) Unfortunately, it is sometimes impossible to get a true picture of how valuable a medium might be to us until we have already become fairly proficient. We sometimes just have to take the plunge.

How to keep up

Here are some suggestions about how to keep up with new information technology.

❑ Assume that you are going to have to keep learning about information technology.

❑ Take an interest in what is becoming available.

❑ Read magazines.

❑ Search the Internet.

❑ Join on-line discussion groups.

❑ Talk with friends and colleagues who use media you are not yet familiar with.

❑ Make friends with colleagues in your organization's IT unit if it has one.

❑ Get people to demonstrate their new systems to you.

❑ Sign up for classes.

❑ Pass on what you have learned to others.

> **KEY IDEA**
>
> With any new technology ask yourself: 'What might it do for my operation that would be worth the costs involved in acquiring, learning and using it'.

Reviewing your information needs

Your information needs may well be constantly changing. The technology for sending and obtaining information certainly is. So don't take your information-handling system for granted. Make a point of reviewing it *regularly* by asking questions of your information *needs* and *sources*.

● What kinds of information do I need?

● Am I getting all the information I need?

● What sources am I currently relying on?

- Are they sufficiently useful, accurate and timely?
- Might there be new or better sources I could tap, for example:
  - libraries, databases, the Internet?
  - networking with new colleagues or peers?
- Would such sources be reasonably cost-effective?
- Am I making best use of the most up-to-date technology?

  Consider how you are *recording* or *storing* information.
- What kinds of information do I need to store, for example:
  - as paper copy?
  - on computer disk?
  - on CD-rom?
  - on an electronic personal organizer?
  - on audio- or videotape?
  - others _____

  _____

- What kinds of information do I need to keep records about, for example:
  - on paper?
  - on computer disk?
  - on CD-Rom?
  - on an electronic personal organizer?
  - on audio- or videotape?
  - others _____

  _____

- When I am recording information, do I do so in appropriate detail?
- Am I always clear about where to store or record different kinds of information and where to find them when they are needed?
- Is my system of recording and storing information reasonably effective and efficient?
- Is it as consistent as it needs to be with those used elsewhere in the organization?
- Is my system understood by everyone who needs to?
- Do I need to ask the above questions about any systems used by members of my staff?

- Do I need to modify our systems in any way?
- Are we making best use of the most up-to-date technology?
- Do I need to arrange relevant training or development for myself or my staff?

  Consider how you are using information.

- Have I been getting information in time to be useful?
- Has it always been presented in the most useful way?
- Have I been giving information in time for it to be useful?
- Have I been getting it to the right people?
- Have I been presenting it in the most appropriate way?
- Has it been getting the results I hoped for?
- How well are my staff using information?
- Are we making best use of the most up-to-date technology?
- If I am less than happy about any of these answers, what can I do to improve matters?

KEY IDEA

Unless it's available in the right form at the right time and place, the best information in the world is valueless.

Managing your career

Contents

Introduction

In the daily thrash of doing well by your job, your team and your organization, don't forget to do well by yourself. You may or may not be staying with this job, this team, this organization. You have your career to think about also. And if you want some influence over your career – rather than just letting it happen to you – then it will take some managing.

The checklists in this chapter urge you to plan your career in terms of what you want out of life. They emphasize the importance of getting worthwhile projects to work on, of making a success of them, and of letting it be *seen* that you are successful. Much of this will depend on how you handle your manager, but you will also need to develop your competences, keep up to date and maintain your integrity. Above all you will need to recognize that no one but you can be relied on to advance your career. So the emphasis here, as throughout this book, is on your *self-development* as a manager.

Planning your career

Your career is an important part of your life. But it is just a part. You will, we hope, go on living after your career is completed. Modern medicine is lengthening many lives, just as modern 'market forces' are shortening many careers. Even while your career is in full swing, you will be spending time on other things as well – family, friends, sport, hobbies, community activity and so on. So managing your career means developing it in line with what you expect from life as a whole.

Few of us ever spend much time thinking about what we want from work. Fewer still consider what we might want from life. Most of us just muddle through both our careers and our lives. Then, quite suddenly, both are almost over and we realize it is too late to achieve our true desires. Those of us who do take stock occasionally, and consider seriously what we really desire, and whether we are prepared to pay the price, are the wise ones. And all it needs is the determination to ask yourself a few simple questions, to be honest in your answers, and to follow through with appropriate action.

- What have been the most satisfying things that have happened in your life so far?

- What have been the most satisfying things that have happened in your career?
- Are there similarities among the things that have given you satisfaction?
- Can you see ways of obtaining similar satisfaction in future?
- What youthful aspirations have you not yet fulfilled?
- Do you still want to fulfil them?
- Are there newer aspirations you want to fulfil?
- How many years do you think you might have left to you?
- What is the best way of using them?

One needs to ask oneself such questions at regular intervals – at least once a year, and additionally whenever one is considering a change of job.

What do you want from life?

Consider the following life aims. Pick out the seven that seem most important to you, and rank those seven from most important (1) to least important (7).

- To earn as much money as possible ❏
- To help people less fortunate than I am ❏
- To enjoy love and companionship ❏
- To have a secure job and an untroubled life ❏
- To have power over other people ❏
- To become as famous as possible ❏
- To be a successful parent and partner to my spouse ❏
- To become an acknowledged expert ❏
- To make worthwhile things or provide a valued service ❏
- To be free of other people's demands ❏
- To do what I believe to be my duty ❏
- To indulge myself having as much pleasure as possible ❏

- To feel that I have stretched myself/fulfilled my potential ❏
- Others _____

_____

How does your career tie in?

- Which of the seven aims you have picked out above might you be able to attain through your present job?

_____

- If there are any you couldn't expect to attain through your present job, might you be able to attain some of those through a different job in management? _____

_____

- If there are some you couldn't expect to attain either through your present job or through another management job, might you be able to attain any of them through a different kind of career altogether? (If so, what?) _____

_____

- Do any of your aims seem to conflict with one another (e.g. the sixth and seventh on the list might do)? _____

_____

- Do the questions above help you to identify any changes you might want to make in your job or your career? (If so, what?) _____

_____

- What would you hope to be doing one year from now? _____

_____

- What would you hope to be doing five years from now? _____

_____

- Does the goal you mention in the last question tie in with the life aims you selected from checklist on page 283? _____

_____

- What sequence of steps would you need to take in order to reach your five-year goal? _____

  _____

- What strengths have you that might help you take those steps? _____

  _____

- What weaknesses have you that might hold you back (unless you can overcome them or compensate for them with your strengths)? _____

  _____

- Can you see any new opportunities that might enable you to get closer to your goal? (What?) _____

  _____

- Can you see any problems that might get in your way? _____

  _____

- What sacrifices might you need to make to attain your goal? (For example, will any of your life aims have to be abandoned?) _____

  _____

- Will such sacrifices be acceptable to you? _____

  _____

- If not, how will you modify your goal? _____

  _____

- How will you measure progress towards your goal? _____

  _____

KEY IDEA

Learn from other people's careers, but don't try to copy any other individual. You are unique and you need to develop your own way of being an effective manager.

Getting on in your job

Whatever plans you have for your career as a whole, the first priority is to make the most of your present job. There are just three main aspects to this:

- Be absolutely clear about what your job **is**.
- Do it **successfully**.
- Be **seen** to be doing it successfully.

What *is* your job?

You may already have worked through the checklists on **Analyzing your job** (page 2). (If not, now would be a good time to do so.) Whether you have or not, here are some points you need to clarify in defining your job.

	Yes	No
● Do I have a job description?	❏	❏
● Whether I do or not, am I clear about what are my chief duties?	❏	❏
● Are any of my duties described in such vague or general terms (e.g. 'staff development') that I and my manager might disagree as to what I am supposed to be doing?	❏	❏
● If so, can I spell out such duties in terms of specific activities – 'give career counselling', 'advise on training courses', 'provide coaching', etc?	❏	❏
● Are all the duties listed really *mine*? ('Spare' duties sometimes creep into a job description merely because they sound like others on the list.)	❏	❏
● Have any important duties been omitted? (If your job is changing, a job description may soon get out of date and need amending.)	❏	❏
● Can I get 'spare' duties removed and new ones recorded?	❏	❏
● Is it clear which duties should occupy most time, and which least?	❏	❏

	Yes	No

- Am I clear about which duties are most critical in terms of cost, benefits and potential embarrassment to my organization? ❏ ❏

- Am I and my manager clearly agreed about any (and all) specific objectives, targets, deadlines, results, etc. that I am expected to achieve? ❏ ❏

- Are my objectives, etc. precise enough that my manager and I should be able to agree as to whether or not they have been achieved? ❏ ❏

- Is it clear how much authority I have to decide priorities, assign staff to jobs, authorize spending and so on? ❏ ❏

- In general, am I sure that my manager and I are agreed about what I should be doing, what authority I have and what results I will be judged by? ❏ ❏

- Am I satisfied that my manager's expectations are reasonable and realistic? ❏ ❏

- Do I feel that, at least for the present, the job is sufficiently 'stretching'? ❏ ❏

If you've answered 'no' to any of the above questions (or weren't sure what to answer), you may have problems doing your present job successfully. Either you aren't entirely satisfied with your job or you aren't as clear as you should be about what is expected of you. Talk this over with your manager. If you haven't got a job description (or it's out of date), draw one up (or revise the old one). Let your manager know:

- what you believe to be the activities you are expected to be engaged in;

- the results you are expected to produce and;

- the authority you are expected to exercise.

And seek your manager's *agreement*, so you both should be able to agree whether you have done the job successfully.

Doing your job successfully

Obviously this whole book is about doing management jobs successfully. But there are a few specific points we need to make here.

- Stick to the job as you have agreed it with your manager.
- Keep your job description where you will see it regularly, and ask yourself:
  - am I carrying out all my duties?
  - am I meeting my objectives?
  - am I exercising (but not exceeding) my authority?
- If extra duties or new objectives arise, discuss them with your manager – not least in terms of how they may interfere with your existing duties and objectives,
- If you take on new duties and objectives (or are relieved of old ones) have this recorded in your agreed job description.
- Cultivate a 'go for it' attitude:
  - set yourself high standards;
  - push yourself to improve on your past performances;
  - don't waste time on inessentials;
  - shrug off failures, and go all the harder for your next objective;
  - respond constructively to constructive criticism;
  - think positively about the future rather than negatively about the past – not 'If only I'd . . .' but 'Next time I will. . .';
  - be flexible and welcoming to new opportunities;
  - look for ways of improving things;
  - be enthusiastic and encourage enthusiasm in those around you;
  - be assertive without being aggressive – and don't alienate those you work with by flaunting your prodigious workrate!
  - be courageous and take calculated risks;
  - work hard to get results (not just to fulfil duties);
  - but watch out for stress and make sure you get enough time off for relaxation.
- Develop your competences. Don't set out hopefully to improve on all fronts at once. Set yourself a new skill to improve in each week, using

the checklists in this book as a guide. For instance, which one of the following areas might you try to improve in first?

When?

– Decision-making	❏	_____
– Planning	❏	_____
– Managing finances	❏	_____
– Controlling	❏	_____
– Interviewing	❏	_____
– Coaching	❏	_____
– Motivating	❏	_____
– Managing my time	❏	_____
– Meetings	❏	_____
– Delegating	❏	_____
– Counselling	❏	_____
– Writing	❏	_____
– Reading	❏	_____
– Listening	❏	_____
– Speaking in public	❏	_____
– Telephoning	❏	_____
– Using information technology	❏	_____
– Negotiating	❏	_____
– Dealing with conflict	❏	_____
– Managing change	❏	_____
– Others	❏	_____

Alongside the area of skill you have chosen to improve in first, make a note of the *week* you are going to do something about it. When you are ready to tackle another area, again note the week alongside.

- Monitor your own work. Keep a work diary in which to make weekly notes about such matters as those I mention below. Which of these might you have made notes about if you had been keeping such a diary over the last 12 months?

– The dates when projects were completed	❏
– The dates when targets or deadlines were met	❏
– Tasks you did particularly well	❏
– Competences you clearly improved	❏

- Things you did less well than you (or your manager)
  would have liked ❑
- Praise or criticism from your manager or from others ❑
- Training or extra help you have had from your
  manager ❑
- Training or extra help that was promised by your
  manager but has not been provided ❑
- Unexpected problems that prevented you from doing
  as well as you might have done, for example: ❑
  - illness ❑
  - staff shortages ❑
  - shortage of money or materials ❑
  - extreme pressures ❑
  - change of duties ❑
  - new objectives/targets/deadlines, etc ❑
  - sudden rushes ❑
  - problems with colleagues ❑
  - problems with clients/customers ❑
  - legal problems ❑
  - others _____

The overall object of this exercise is to make sure that your memory of your work – and the success with which you are doing your job and improving your competences – is at least as sound (and preferably sounder) than that of your manager. This may be vital if you have an annual performance appraisal.

Being seen to work successfully

It is not enough to know your job and do it well. You must also be seen to do it well. VISIBILITY is the name of the game. This doesn't mean you have to go around bragging about how brilliant you are. But it does mean that you must not be unduly modest and assume that such virtue as yours simply cannot go unnoticed and unrewarded. It can and it will, unless you bring it to people's attention.

- Be open and confident about your work in talking to other people around the organization.

- Talk to your manager regularly about your work.

- Make sure he or she has noticed your successes and improvements. (This applies especially to women, for women are generally more hesitant than men about drawing attention to their achievements.)

- Send your manager a brief note recording the completion of all major projects or objectives.

- Ask your manager for an opinion as to how you are doing on some of your main duties – especially those that have given problems in the past and in which you know you have now improved.

- Point out the extra training or other steps you have taken to improve your performance.

- Never express doubts as to your ability to quickly *acquire* whatever competences are needed, even if you must admit that you don't have them all just yet.

- Consider seeking accreditation for managerial competences you have already acquired.

- However you present yourself, and whatever you say to your manager and other people around the organization, remember that folks are usually pretty willing to believe we are what we tell them we are – provided there is no blatant evidence to the contrary.

- Don't moan to your manager about difficulties you are facing or blame your shortcomings on other people.

- Modestly pass on to your manager (especially if he/she is likely to see it as reflecting well on the section as a whole) any praise you receive from elsewhere in the organization or from outside.

- If you are looking to earn promotion, make sure your manager knows this. (Women, in particular, are often passed over for promotion because they have not made their ambitions clear.)

Appraisal interviews

Perhaps you will be given official appraisal interviews at regular intervals. If so this may present you with a particularly powerful opportunity to convince or remind your manager that you are doing your job successfully. To make the most of such an opportunity you will need to prepare for it thoughtfully and then handle the actual interview to your best advantage.

- You can best prepare for an appraisal interview by jotting down answers to questions such as these.
  - What have I done most effectively and/or with greatest satisfaction since my last appraisal?
  - What have I done least effectively and/or with least satisfaction during that period?
  - Have I come across any obstacles – in my own knowledge and skills or in the working conditions – that have prevented me from working as effectively or with as much satisfaction as I would have wished?
  - What are my main strengths?
  - What are my main weaknesses?
  - Is there any way my job might be improved (both to my benefit and that of the section) to enable me to spend a greater proportion of my time on the sort of work I do most effectively and with greatest satisfaction?
  - If I were in charge of my manager's team, what changes would I want to make in the way things are done?
  - In order to increase both my job satisfaction and my team's productivity in the months ahead, what new things might need to be done by:
    - me?
    - my manager (or other managers)?
    - anyone else?
  - If such things were done, what should I be able to achieve in the coming months that I have not been able to achieve since the last appraisal?
  - During my appraisal interview, are there any other issues I would like to discuss, for example:
    - my present duties?
    - my special interests and competences?
    - my ambitions?
    - my training needs?
    - my needs for extra resources or support?

     – others   _____

     – What would I like to happen as a result of the appraisal interview?

- During your appraisal interview, concentrate on building up your manager's confidence in your present performance and your potential for the future.
  - Get across your views about your job and how you perform it.
  - Draw attention to your successes and achievements (using your work diary as a reminder if necessary).
  - But don't suggest these are due to your being a superior sort of person. (Leave that conclusion for your manager to come to.)
  - Mention any tributes you've received from people known to and respected by your manager – but only if you can do so without seeming to be crowing.
  - Give sincere credit to any circumstances that have favoured you or to people who have helped you succeed.
  - Be proud without being arrogant.
  - Be self-assured without being bumptious.
  - But don't:
    - tell outright lies;
    - exaggerate;
    - blind the manager with jargon;
    - pretend ignorance of mistakes;
    - pooh-pooh your manager's concern;
    - blame everyone but yourself.
  - Listen actively to your manager's words (and look out for body language and other non-verbal signals).
  - Do your best to find out what is going on in his or her mind.
  - Respond appropriately, for example if your manager makes a comment or asks a question you don't understand, ask for it to be explained.
  - If you understand the question but don't know the answer, admit it, don't flannel.
  - Don't take all comments/questions to mean exactly what they say. For example 'Tell me what you've been doing all year' is not really an invitation to reminisce for three hours.
  - Even if the manager does mean it (e.g. 'How do you get on with Mr So-and-So?') you may decide not to be too frank.

- Look out for assumptions, beliefs or prejudices that lie behind your manager's statements, e.g. 'No problems with customer complaints this year, I see'.
- If you think the underlying beliefs etc. are mistaken (you've never had customer complaints as far as you know), challenge the statement and ask your manager what events he or she is thinking of.
- Watch out especially for remarks that might indicate your manager is taking you less than seriously on account of your:
  - race;
  - religion;
  - sex;
  - marital status;
  - age;
  - country of birth;
  - regional accent;
  - physical handicap;
  - length of time in the organization;
  - personal antipathy, etc.
- If you feel that your manager is prejudiced, you may wish to ask for your appraisal interview to be carried out by someone else. (And see **Managing equal opportunities**, page 84.)
- If you have to face criticism:
  - Listen as coolly as you can, without interruption.
  - Establish exactly what is being criticized. Don't put up with generalities, e.g. 'Your whole attitude's altogether wrong'. Ask politely for specific examples.
  - Try to be objective – can you see the truth of the criticism?
  - If you think it's unfair or ill-founded, don't just deny it. Try instead to remind your manager of *contradictory* evidence, e.g. 'Would you have said that of me the other week when...?'
  - If the criticism is based on faulty memory or a mistake, gently put the record straight.
  - Don't attack your manager for being stupid or prejudiced (even if you believe it). Remain calm and dignified (at least on the surface) – you need to keep your wits about you.

– Don't offer excuses or suggest the fault doesn't matter – but do make clear you have *learned* from its occurrence.

– Encourage your manager to discuss with you what can be done to overcome the fault or shortcoming, making sure you have some ideas of your own to offer.

– Aim to work the conversation around to your strengths and the ways in which you are doing your work satisfactorily.

– Make sure that both you and your manager are clear what both of you have agreed to do as a result of the appraisal interview in order to build on your strengths and overcome your weaknesses – so that your next appraisal will reveal you as being even more successful in doing your job.

● In the months following your appraisal interview, make sure your manager is aware that you are doing what was agreed – and be even more assiduous in applying the 12 points on page 249.

KEY IDEA

By visibly doing your work successfully you are likely to be offered promotion. But beware of the so-called 'Peter principle' – that eventually everyone tends to get promoted to a level where they are no longer competent (and where they no longer enjoy their work).

Managing your manager

Books on management have plenty of advice on how to manage your staff. But they seem to have little or nothing to say about how to manage your manager. Yet all managers have managers of their own, and usually he or she determines not only how satisfied and effective they are in their present jobs but also how easily they can move ahead in their careers.

If you want to get the best out of your manager, you can't afford just to sit back and assume that he or she can be trusted to look after your best interests. Not all are that caring; many who may care are not competent enough; and many who are competent are too busy furthering their own careers.

Yet there is a lot you can do to make a good situation better and a bad situation less bad. At least you can take action to avoid being exploited or overlooked.

It's your manager's job to manage your work. But if you want to survive being managed, you need to manage your manager. This means getting him or her to:

- Notice you;
- Respect you;
- Acknowledge your strengths;
- Allow you to influence his or her decisions;
- Help you progress towards your own goals;
- Deal with you fairly and honestly;
- Make your working life tolerable/productive for you;
- Keep you out of messes;
- Avoid getting in your way or making a fool of you.

In short, it means influencing the way he or she sees you and behaves towards you. The checklists in this section consider ways of doing this. You may also want to look at those on **Getting on in your job** (page 244) – especially the one concerning 'Being *seen* to work successfully'.

Problems with managers

- Some lucky people do not have any particular problems with their managers. Others are not so fortunate. Do you have any of the following problems – some of the many that managers have mentioned to me?
  - 'My manager ignores me'   ❏
  - 'My manager distrusts me'   ❏
  - 'My manager keeps me in the dark about what I am
    supposed to be doing or achieving'   ❏
  - 'My manager is inconsistent about what is expected
    of me'   ❏

- 'My manager makes decisions that affect the work of my staff without consulting me' ❑
- 'My manager used to do my job and finds it difficult to accept that I want to do it differently' ❑
- 'My manager is too busy currying favour with superiors to bother with subordinates like me' ❑
- 'My manager doesn't involve me sufficiently in the important planning and decision-making' ❑
- 'My manager is never around when needed' ❑
- 'My manager has favourites ('drinking cronies') and if you're not one of them you're a nobody' ❑
- 'My manager is weak and ineffectual in fighting for our department's resources and reputation' ❑
- 'My manager doesn't give my ideas the encouragement I believe they deserve' ❑
- 'My manager is always quick to criticize ('keeping us on our toes') but rarely gives praise' ❑
- 'My manager is too worried about us making mistakes and drawing down the wrath of the powers-that-be to risk doing something innovative that might actually win us some Brownie points' ❑
- 'My manager doesn't delegate properly' ❑
- 'My manager is pig-headed, domineering and liable to get violent (verbally if not physically)' ❑
- 'My manager goes in for sexual harassment' ❑
- 'I'm not sure who my real manager is' ❑
- Others _____

_____

- ● Can you be sure that none of your staff would make any such remarks about you? ❑

In some of the cases listed above, the manager is clearly a very difficult person to deal with. In most cases, however, it seems likely that the one doing the complaining is not doing all that might be done to establish a more congenial and productive relationship. The following checklists give some guidance in creating such relationships.

Know your manager

If you are to handle your manager to best advantage you'll need to know a fair bit about him or her. Some people, as shown in the last comment in the checklist above, are not even sure who their 'real' manager is. If you report to more than one person, then you may need to answer such questions as the following for all of them.

- What are your manager's likes and dislikes?
- What are your manager's prejudices and idiosyncrasies?
- What is your manager's personal and professional history?
- Is he or she married, with or without children?
- What clubs, associations, outside activities is your manager involved with? (Can you honestly share an interest in any of these?)
- What is your manager's circle of friends, inside and outside the organization?
- How is he or she regarded by other people (especially the influential people) in the organization?
- What are his or her strengths and weaknesses as a manager?
- What styles of leadership does your manager favour (see the checklists on **Developing leadership**, page 95)?
- What motivates your manager?
- What personal ambitions does your manager have?
- What, if anything, does he or she fear or have anxieties about?
- What does your manager expect from you?
- In which of the following ways do you think of your manager?
    - Friend ❑
    - Equal colleague ❑
    - Senior colleague ❑
    - Advisor/mentor ❑
    - A liability ❑
    - Judge ❑
    - Slave driver ❑
    - Oppressor ❑

		Yes	No

- Competitor   ❏
- Opponent   ❏
- Others _____

	Yes	No
● Does your manager think of you in a way that matches your view of your manager? (If your manager thinks of you as someone he or she is grooming for advancement and you think of your manager as someone you are competing with for promotion, your working relationship can hardly be as honest as it ought to be.)	❏	❏

Supporting your manager

The baseline for managing your manager is to let him or her know that you can be relied on – not only to do your own job but also to support your manager in doing his or her job.

- Be available.

- Impress upon your manager (quietly but frequently) that you are doing your job successfully. (See the checklists on **Getting on in your job**, page 244.)

- Encourage your manager to talk to you about his or her problems.

- Try to see your manager's problems through his or her eyes.

- Anticipate your manager's needs, priorities and expectations (even if unspoken).

- Volunteer to take some of the load off your manager's shoulders where appropriate.

- Help your manager to realize that you have strengths that can compensate for his or her weaknesses – and are thus a valuable, if not indispensable, ally in attaining his or her goals.

- Make it clear, if appropriate, that you can help your manager to avoid or overcome whatever he or she fears or is anxious about.

- When projects do get delegated to you by your manager, see them through to completion. Don't turn in a half-baked job with all the tricky bits left for your manager to tidy up.

- Speak well of your manager to others and be as loyal as you would wish him or her to be to you.

- Present yourself as working *with*, rather than *for* your manager – and make a point of disagreeing (politely) from time to time, if only to make it clear that you are not a yes-person.

- But don't be too proud to express admiration for your manager, if you are lucky enough to have one who deserves it, perhaps by adopting what you take to be his or her admirable features and by asking for advice.

- Keep your promises.

- Be equally honest and collaborative with your colleagues and fellow managers so that you don't get mistrusted as the office creep or the manager's pet.

Getting your manager's support

You give your manager support, and you expect support in return. Here's how to get it.

- Make a friend of your manager's secretary or assistant – for he or she will be able to help you in many ways.

- Find out how your manager likes proposals to be presented, e.g. in a written document or in a leisurely face-to-face discussion.

- When is the best time to approach your manager – what time of day, what day of the week?

- Where is the best place to tackle your manager – in the office, over lunch, in the park?

- Present your proposals in such a way that your manager can contribute to them and thus feel some 'ownership' in them.

- Show your manager how he or she can gain something of value from what you are proposing. (See the checklists on **Negotiating**, page 38.)

- Don't force your manager into a situation where it is clear that you can only gain what you want at his or her expense. Ensure at least that your manager takes no risk without some chance of gain.

- If your manager makes suggestions that are at all practicable, incorporate them into your proposal.

- If they are not practicable, get your manager talking about the implications until *he/she* decides they are not.

- If your manager offers a better proposal altogether, acclaim it as such and be the one to offer suggestions.

- If the only way of getting your ideas adopted is to let your manager believe they were his/her own, you may *sometimes* decide to go along with this for the sake of the proposal – but don't do it as a matter of course, or your creativity may never get the recognition it deserves.

- Don't try too many new ideas on your manager all at once; you can always come back with additional proposals another day, once you've earned your manager's confidence.

- If your manager comes up with strong objections to the proposal, argue your case as strongly as you can without seeming fanatical, but don't try to bludgeon him or her into submission. Go away and think about your proposal and come back another day with a modified and, hopefully, more acceptable version.

When you have problems

- Don't bother your manager with minor problems you can sort out yourself, perhaps with the aid of a colleague.

- If your manager must get to hear about problems you are having, make sure he or she hears it from you first.

- Don't let your manager be embarrassed (e.g. with his or her manager) by having to admit ignorance of an impending crisis (yours) in the department.

- If something is going seriously wrong, tell your manager what has happened, why it has happened and suggest ways you might deal with the problem.

- Don't waste time on excuses and buck-passing – and if you think your manager is to blame, keep the thought to yourself.

- Invite your manager's views and suggestions, but on no account act as though you expect your manager to solve the problem for you.

- Without desperately overworking the 'first the bad news, now the good news' approach, do try to find some aspect of the situation for your manager and you to be positive and optimistic about.

- Be honest and open, admit your mistakes and don't try to mislead your manager. Better a brief rollocking than to be permanently thought of as devious and untrustworthy.

- If you both know that you are to blame, make it clear that you have learned from the experience and will be unlikely to repeat your error.

- Steer your manager into planning with you for the future rather than moaning about what is in the past.

- Make sure you don't err in the same way again.

When your manager *is* the problem

As we noticed in the problems mentioned by managers in the checklist on page 254, some managers are problems in themselves. They may be incompetent, paranoid, uninterested, unreasonable, manipulative, greedy, bad-tempered, alcoholic or sexually rapacious. Such managers are a small minority (as far as we know), but that's no comfort if one of them is yours. How can they be managed?

- Make sure that all dealings you have with such a manager are recorded in writing (e.g. in memos or in a personal diary) – especially if you suspect that your manager may deny or distort what has taken place or been discussed between you.

- If you feel your manager has let you down (e.g. in undermining your authority or failing to provide some promised support), do let him or her know that you feel let down. (They are sometimes honestly oblivious to the hurt they have caused.)

- Don't get into shouting matches with your manager (let alone physical conflicts). At all costs, keep your temper. (See the checklists on **Managing conflict**, page 152.)

- Discuss your manager with fellow managers, discover whether they feel as badly treated as you do and what they have done about it or what, together, you might plan to do about it.

- Consult your colleagues in informal networks around the organization to learn more about how your manager is seen and whether anyone has ever found ways of effectively dealing with his or her undesirable behaviour.

- Consider consulting your manager's manager (provided the two are not in cahoots) – preferably in company with others who feel as you do, and preferably in a manner that will be seen as attempting to solve a problem for the sake of the organization rather than the young bloods trying to oust the old guard.

- If your manager's manager is not to be trusted, consider asking advice from some other influential person with a good reputation in the organization.

- Consider any machinery that exists for making an official complaint (such as the personnel department).

- Consider involving your professional association or trade union.

- Where you believe that your manager is offending against the laws of the land, or even just the rules of the organization (e.g. sexual or racial discrimination, health and safety regulations, sexual harassment) you may need to put a documented case to the highest level of management.

- In desperation, you may be able to plot with your colleagues to play on your manager's fears or weaknesses in order to bring about his or her exposure and downfall. (But this is always a risky business and more than likely to rebound on the virtuous plotters, leaving the villain unscathed.)

- In the end you may decide that the best way of managing an unmanageable manager is to leave him or her (even if you have to take a drop in pay or status in going to a more congenial post elsewhere).

> **KEY IDEA**
>
> If any of your staff are managers (or aspiring to be), they too may have read this section. So please be understanding of their attempts to manage you.

Developing your competences

In recent years, vocational trainers around the world have been talking in terms of *competences* – the skills and abilities, backed up by knowledge and understanding, that enable a person to perform well in a particular type of job or profession. First of all, there are general (generic) competences that will benefit one in almost any profession, for example the ability to think laterally or to learn from experience. Then there are the specific competences that make for capability in a particular occupation.

What general competences might you need?

I will leave you to follow up on the management standards, if you are interested and haven't already done so. It might be interesting for you to think about how relevant they seem to the kind of management in which you are involved. Meanwhile you may like to consider the more general competences listed below. These would help you to be more effective as a manager, as they would in other areas of your life. Consider whether you rate as average, above average or below average (compared with other managers you know) on each of these general competences.

	Below	Average	Above
• *Technical/professional knowledge*			
How up-to-date are you in your knowledge of the product or service your organization (or section) provides?	❏	❏	❏
• *Organisational know-how*			
How clued up are you about your organization's policies, plans, priorities,			

	Below	Average	Above
personalities, power struggles, politics, problems and outside reputation?	❏	❏	❏

● *Ability to grasp a situation*

How quick are you at separating the relevant from the irrelevant in a new situation and seeing through to the heart of the matter?   ❏   ❏   ❏

● *Decision-making ability*

How confident are you of your ability to analyze situations and make appropriate decisions fast enough?   ❏   ❏   ❏

● *Creativity*

Are you able to come up with original, intuitive solutions to problems?   ❏   ❏   ❏

● *Mental flexibility*

Can you juggle with more than one problem at a time, perhaps with conflicting data to handle, and still think fast?   ❏   ❏   ❏

● *Proactivity*

Are you ready to take the initiative in making things happen rather than waiting for them to happen to you?   ❏   ❏   ❏

● *Moral courage*

Have you the guts to take what may be an unpopular line of action because you expect it to produce a worthwhile result?   ❏   ❏   ❏

● *Resilience*

How well do you cope with uncertainty, tension, stress, fatigue and other people's hostility or unreasonable demands?   ❏   ❏   ❏

● *Social skills*

Can you get on productively with other people, whether you are being sympathetic

	Below	Average	Above
and supportive or are handling conflict or hostility and being assertive?	❏	❏	❏

- *Self-knowledge*

Do you make a practice of examining your own goals, beliefs and values and considering why you feel and behave the way you do?   ❏ ❏ ❏

- *The ability to learn from experience*

Do you make a practice of reflecting on incidents at work, weighing up the actions of yourself and others involved, and considering how you might handle such people or incidents in future?   ❏ ❏ ❏

Few of us will be above average on all 12 qualities or abilities. Even if you are, you may decide you are not *sufficiently* above average. That is, you may feel the need for greater organizational know-how or social skills or whatever. Circle your ticks in the boxes above for the *three* abilities you would most like to improve.

Improving your competences

How can you develop those competences that will aid you in your career as a manager? On the one hand, you can look to people to teach you. On the other hand, you can take responsibility for your own learning. (And, of course, you can combine the two approaches.)

Here are some sources from which you may be able to obtain more or less formal teaching. Which of them do you think might be able to help you with the abilities you want to improve?

- Coaching from your manager   ❏
- Sessions/courses run by your own organization   ❏
- Visits from training consultants   ❏
- Local colleges or/universities   ❏
- Regional management centres   ❏

- Business schools ❏
- Commercial training organizations ❏
- Professional institutions ❏
- Trade unions ❏
- Government-funded schemes ❏
- Industry training boards ❏
- Employers' federations ❏
- Correspondence colleges ❏
- Open learning/distance teaching providers ❏
- Others _____

Now for some self-development, or do-it-yourself, approaches. Which of the following look like ways in which you might improve the competences you need as a manager?

- Go and introduce yourself to members of staff you don't normally meet and get them to tell you about their work and the problems they face ❏
- Join a committee to do with some aspect of the organization's business that is new to you ❏
- Get yourself seconded to another branch of your organization or another section within your branch ❏
- Take on some additional part-time work in another part of your organization, e.g. acting as club treasurer or helping run the crèche ❏
- Ask friends and acquaintances elsewhere to invite you to visit their organizations ❏
- Join some voluntary group in your community in which you can experiment with social skills in a way you might not care to risk at work ❏
- Change one of the ways in which you deal with people in your organization, perhaps following the guidelines given in some of the checklists in this book ❏

- Get feedback from members of your team, from your manager and from fellow managers ❑
- Pick out someone who clearly has the competences you want to develop; observe them in operation and get them to discuss those competences ❑
- Similarly, be prepared to act as a 'role model' yourself for colleagues who see you as having competences they would like to improve ❑
- Take time to read professional journals and books that you don't normally bother with ❑
- Make a point of mentioning to your colleagues anything you've read that may interest them ❑
- Write articles on your work, your organization or your organization's area of activity ❑
- Look for opportunities to speak to local groups about your work and organization ❑
- Attend conferences and seminars relating to your work and make an input to them ❑
- Keep a journal of 'critical incidents' at work (there's got to be at least one a week!) recording what happened, how you felt and acted, and what you learned from it ❑
- Try writing some short stories or a novel about what happens at work (but don't worry if they are never polished enough to offer for publication!) ❑
- Apply in your family and social life some of the management skills you acquire in your work ❑
- Apply at work some of the expectations and approaches you use with your family and friends ❑
- Spend some time every day reading a serious novel or book of biography, travel or whatever, that has no obvious connection with your work ❑
- Nurture some outside interest (anything from local politics to vintage car restoration) that is just as absorbing as your work ❑

- Others _____

_____

Clearly not all the approaches above will suit everyone. But all have profited some. No doubt you will be able to think of other methods of your own by which you can develop the competences you need as a manager.

> **KEY IDEA**
>
> If you work in the UK, consider going for an N/SVQ in management or, wherever you are, consider taking a part-time certificate, diploma or degree course in the subject.

Keeping up to date

Are you prepared to learn new ways? 'The times, they are a-changing . . .' sang Bob Dylan in the 1960s – and that was before they invented information technology! The effective manager is one who keeps an eye on the emerging trends (and sudden shifts) in society – and is ready to adapt to them.

In whatever field of activity you are managing – in industry, in the retail trade, in tourism, in the civil service, in education, in banking and finance, in the police service or whatever – your organization will constantly be facing change, and your role cannot avoid being affected. Public tastes and expectations change. Governments change. The law changes. Technology changes. People's attitudes to work change. Products and services change. The people you are working with change. And you are getting older, so you are changing. But are you prepared to manage your personal change in such a way as to keep up to date with the changing world?

It's not easy – especially when change is so rapid and one is already running as fast as one can (or is it merely as fast as one feels like running?) just to stay in the same place. There is also the temptation to be cynical and dismissive. We managers who've been around a while can be inclined to say 'It's just another gimmick/bandwagon/temporary hiccup/imaginary hurdle . . . We've seen it all before . . . I'll give it six months. . .It'll soon settle itself down again . . . There'll be a different bunch of trendsetters along any day now . . .', and so on.

But some changes just cannot be wished away. We've all seen markets disappear, jobs disappear, departments disappear and whole organizations changed out of all recognition. Such changes need to be foreseen and evaluated in terms of what we must do to control or adapt to them, and to work out appropriate ways of changing ourselves accordingly. If we don't we shall be supplanted by people who do.

So the checklists in this section are here to remind you of the need to 'hang loose' in your thinking (don't get stuck in a groove) and to regard change as a possible source of opportunities rather than of problems only.

What changes have you seen?

- What are the three biggest changes that have happened in your organization within the last 12 months? _____

  _____

- What caused these changes? _____

  _____

- Did these changes affect your job or the jobs of people you have to work with? _____

  _____

- Did you have to adopt any new ways of working? _____

  _____

- If so, have you done so satisfactorily? _____

  _____

- Were there problems in learning new ways? _____

  _____

- How much advance warning did you have that change was coming? _____

  _____

- Would longer advance warning have made learning the new ways any easier? _____

  _____

- Can you predict the next three important changes that are likely to affect your organization (or your section)? _____

  _____

- Can you see how you may have to change your ways as a result? _____

  _____

- Do you think you are doing enough already to anticipate and prepare for change? (If 'yes', are you quite, quite sure?) _____

  _____

Preparing for change

Here are some questions to ask yourself, expanding on the last question in the list above.

Using published information

	Yes	No
Do you read a 'quality' daily newspaper?	❏	❏
Do you regularly read the technical/ professional journals in your field?	❏	❏
Have you read a book on management (apart from this one) within the last 12 months?	❏	❏
Have you read a *recently published* book on management (apart from this one) within the last 12 months?	❏	❏
Could you mention the key works that have been published in your field in the last 12 months?	❏	❏
If not, would you know how to find out?	❏	❏
Do you know what published information is stored within your organization and how to get access to it?	❏	❏
Do you know of any computer databases that contain information relevant to your field?	❏	❏
Do you know where and how to use them?	❏	❏

	Yes	No
• Have you, within the last 12 months, requested information on technical or management matters from government departments, professional associations, etc?	❑	❑
• Could you, without preparation, give one of your junior colleagues a rundown on current professional issues?	❑	❑
• Do you regularly watch TV programmes or listen to radio programmes about current affairs, social trends and technological developments?	❑	❑

Training and education

	Yes	No
• Do you regularly obtain details of forthcoming courses, workshops, conferences, seminars, etc. that might be helpful to you in updating your technical or professional competence?	❑	❑
• Have you thought in the last six months about what training or development opportunities you might particularly welcome to help you update yourself?	❑	❑
• If so, have you made any attempts to obtain such opportunities?	❑	❑
• Have you attended an updating course, workshop, seminar, etc. within the last six months?	❑	❑
• Have you started on any open/distance learning course about management, e.g. the diploma, certificate or MBA courses of The Open University's Open Business School?	❑	❑

Exchanging information

	Yes	No
• Do you seek to obtain new ideas from your own staff?	❑	❑
• Do you encourage your staff to keep themselves up to date?	❑	❑
• Do you regularly exchange updating information with colleagues elsewhere in the organization?	❑	❑

	Yes	No
● Do you study the activities of other organizations in your field?	❏	❏
● Have you recently visited any other organizations in your field or a related field?	❏	❏
● Are you an *active* member of a professional body?	❏	❏
● Have you sought the advice of any experts in your field within the last 12 months?	❏	❏
● Do you know of universities or other research bodies carrying out research of relevance to your field?	❏	❏
● Do you know how to obtain information about the findings of such research?	❏	❏
● Are you aware of any relevant advisory services offered by government departments or independent organizations?	❏	❏
● Are you the kind of person colleagues would look to for reliable information about what's new?	❏	❏

If your answer to many of the above questions is 'no', then it's doubtful if you are doing all you should to keep reasonably up to date. You may like to consider which of the above steps you might take in order to be able to rate yourself as more up to date next time you read through this checklist.

What changes may be coming?

Here are just a few of the trends I have noticed in recent times. I expect you could easily add to the list. Which of them do you believe are relevant – either already or in the future – for you, your organization, your work within it, or the kind of manager you want to be?

● A shift from producing goods to producing, processing and distributing information	❏
● The growth of personal-service activities – counselling, health and beauty care, tourism, etc.	❏

- The need to be responsive to challenges (e.g. in markets, in new labour sources or in new competition) from countries anywhere in the world ❏

- A smaller and smaller proportion of the population having lifetime careers ❏

- A shift from centralized decision-making towards decentralisation, devolution and greater local autonomy ❏

- A shift from organizational provision of goods and services towards self-help and 'do-it-yourself' ❏

- A shift from permanent hierarchies at work towards a more flexible use of temporary groups drawn together specifically to tackle particular projects with a fixed duration ❏

- Both individuals and organizations having a vastly greater range of options to choose from than they have ever had before ❏

- The increasing use by organizations of freelance professional services rather than salaried staff ❏

- A shift towards the voluntary (unpaid) sector as an area in which to find satisfying work ❏

- The need for frequent retraining or continuous professional development in order to remain employable ❏

- Opportunities provided by the Internet to become a self-employed entrepreneur, working from home but operating world-wide, on minimal capital investment ❏

- Others _____

KEY IDEA

If you don't prepare yourself to manage for the future, you may soon find you are a manager of the past.

Maintaining your integrity

Throughout this book the emphasis in the checklists is on thinking rationally, making appropriate decisions and behaving effectively. One of the prime aims of effective management is not just to do things right but to do the right things. But what do we mean by right? Is it merely a matter of getting what you *want* for yourself, your team or your organization? Or does it raise questions of conscience, morality and ethics – of whether what you are doing is fair, decent and honourable?

Most people assume that different areas of activity have different ethical standards. For example, used-car traders (like the horse traders who preceded them) were once thought to be, in general, rather less honourable in their dealings than, say, the people in medical care and banking. But the courts and the news media have been revealing medical cover-ups and financial scams for long enough now to throw such assumptions into question.

The cynics among us may say 'They're all at it – it's just that organizations with a suave, professional image are less likely to be found out'. The realists will say that while even the most public-spirited fields of activity have their occasional bad apples, the most shady trades have the occasional individual who is struggling to do the decent thing.

What sort of ethical standards prevail in your field of activity and in your particular organization? Are there boundaries of fair play beyond which people just wouldn't go in dealing with suppliers and competitors? Are the rights and dignities of your clients or customers respected? Do staff at least aim to act honourably towards one another? Or is it a case of 'We've got to do it to them before they do it to us' and 'Never give the punters an even break' and 'We can't afford to be too honest'? How do your own ethical standards compare with those current in your organization? And how easily can you maintain your integrity?

What is ethically acceptable in your organization?

Here are a number of practices that managers have mentioned to me as having happened within their organizations. Put a tick in the first box alongside any that you think would be regarded as ethically acceptable by most people in your organization.

	Yes	No
• Misleading customers or clients about the exact nature or quality of what they will be getting for their money	❏	❏
• Finding imaginative ways of charging customers or clients more than they were expecting to pay	❏	❏
• Persuading suppliers to give you special deals because alternative suppliers (so you pretend) have offered them	❏	❏
• Offering 'personal financial inducements' to individuals in other organizations to persuade them to give your organization preferential treatment	❏	❏
• Delaying the payment of suppliers for as long as is possible without incurring legal penalties	❏	❏
• Finding ways of paying less tax than the organization really should be paying	❏	❏
• Obtaining public funds to which the organization is not really entitled	❏	❏
• Reducing the price of the organization's goods or services below what is charged by a competitor, and taking a loss for a while, in order to drive that competitor out of business	❏	❏
• Promoting false stories about competitors in order to lose them business	❏	❏
• Having people infiltrate the competitors in order to discover their commercial secrets	❏	❏
• Obtaining personal (e.g. financial or sexual) information about customers, suppliers or the organization's own staff without their knowledge	❏	❏
• Making an offer he or she could not refuse to one of your competitor's staff whose departure would gravely damage them and/or much enhance your operation	❏	❏
• Withholding information from members of staff that might have led them to behave in ways inconvenient to the manager, the section or the organization	❏	❏

	Yes	No
• Promising colleagues favours that one has no intention of giving them	❏	❏
• Inviting colleagues to co-operate with one in return for not making public certain delicate information one has about them	❏	❏
• Fabricating a case against colleagues with whom people dislike working in order to justify getting them dismissed	❏	❏
• Taking advantage of current employment or supply conditions to persuade people to accept less pay than would normally be due to them	❏	❏
• Inflating personal expense accounts	❏	❏
• Taking home items of the organization's products	❏	❏
• Doing private business in the organization's time	❏	❏
• Engaging in any practice of advantage to the individual manager, the section or the organization – however dubious – so long as there is no possibility of its becoming known to people who might object	❏	❏
• Others _____		

Your own ethical standards

- Put a tick in the second box alongside any of the practices in the above checklist that *you personally* think might be acceptable (at least sometimes).

- Have there been any occasions in the past six months when you have done things that would be regarded as ethically unacceptable in your organization?

- Have there been occasions when you have done things which would be generally accepted as ethical within the organization, but which you felt guilty or uncomfortable about doing?

- Have there been occasions when you deliberately resisted doing something which would be generally acceptable but which was unethical by your own standards?

- Overall, do you feel that you are inclined to be rather more or rather less ethical than the general standards in your organization?
- Would colleagues treat you with any suspicion, derision or hostility if your ethical standards were obviously different from theirs?
- Which of the following has the greatest and least influence on your ethical behaviour at work? Rank them in order from 1 (greatest) to 6 (least).
    - The rules and regulations of the organization ❑
    - The standards prevailing in my field generally ❑
    - My personal beliefs and values ❑
    - Pressures from people in my team ❑
    - The way my fellow managers behave ❑
    - The advice and behaviour of my manager ❑

However strong one's personal beliefs and values, it is very difficult to remain totally unaffected by the behaviour of those around one. In some organizations the person with a conscience may even find that it is necessary to 'do good by stealth' in order to avoid being thought a candidate for sainthood (or a knife in the back!).

Questioning your own actions

When business is slack, competition is ruthless and resources are constantly being eroded, there are many temptations to cut ethical corners and get what one needs by any means possible. Fortunately most managers are able to resist that temptation – either because their conscience won't let them or because they recognize it as a slippery slope that will sooner or later lead both them and their organization into disrepute. Maintaining one's integrity, and thereby justifying other people's trust, is not just good ethics, it's also good management.

If you ever do suspect that you are being tempted into actions that might compromise your integrity, these are the kinds of conscience-jogging questions you might usefully ask yourself. (If you can, try relating them to some recent decision or action that troubled your conscience at the time.)

	Yes	No
• Would I be able to do this to the people I am doing it to if they knew why I was really doing it?	❏	❏
• Am I acting towards these people as if their feelings, needs and interests are just as important as my own?	❏	❏
• Am I certain that other people (e.g. my manager) are not using me to serve their purposes and needs without regard for my own?	❏	❏
• Would I be happy if what I propose doing to members of my staff or colleagues were to be done to me by my colleagues or my manager?	❏	❏
• Would I think it acceptable for members of my staff to act in this fashion?	❏	❏
• Would I feel such behaviour was acceptable in a competitor?	❏	❏
• Would I find anything to complain about if my worst enemy acted this way?	❏	❏
• Would I be happy about such behaviour becoming universal in my organization or field of activity?	❏	❏
• Even though 'everyone else' is thought to be acting this way, would I still feel easy about doing it if *no one* else did?	❏	❏
• Even though my individual action is not doing much harm, could I still say the same if everyone decided to act like me?	❏	❏
• Would I feel able to justify my action and motives to an impartial committee of inquiry?	❏	❏
• Could I justify them to my spouse, best friends or children?	❏	❏
• Could I behave in this way towards my spouse, best friends or children?	❏	❏
• Would I be happy for my actions and motives to be discussed during the evening's television news or an investigative programme?	❏	❏

	Yes	No
• Would I be able to live with the kind of person I might become if I made a practice of such behaviour?	❑	❑

> **KEY IDEA**
>
> The old motto 'Do unto others as you would be done by' is still the most practical guide to ethical behaviour that a manager can follow.

Your monthly check-up

Just to make sure that you keep managing as well as you know how, you may find it useful to check on yourself at least once a month. Reflect on what you have been doing, using questions like these – plus any others you can think of that will apply particularly to your situation.

Since I last worked through this checklist, have I:

	Yes	No
• Attained whatever goals or targets I was planning to attain by this date?	❑	❑
• Clarified my goals or targets for the next six months?	❑	❑
• Made adequate plans towards attaining my current goals and targets?	❑	❑
• Decided what I want to achieve at work during the coming week?	❑	❑
• Kept in mind what I want to attain over the next five years?	❑	❑
• Kept in mind what I want to achieve in the rest of my life?	❑	❑
• Done things and produced results that contribute to attaining my long-term plans?	❑	❑
• Concentrated on what I know to be important rather than on what is easier to do or more immediately rewarding?	❑	❑
• Been judging myself by what I have achieved rather than by how hard I have been working?	❑	❑

	Yes	No
● Stopped any unproductive activities?	❏	❏
● Made myself spend adequate time on planning?	❏	❏
● Been delegating as much work as possible?	❏	❏
● Been systematic in monitoring (controlling) the work of my team?	❏	❏
● Ever reminded myself of the cost of my time?	❏	❏
● Taken steps to improve the way I manage my time?	❏	❏
● Taken any necessary steps to ensure that work pressures have not become unduly stressful?	❏	❏
● Done all I could to make the working lives of my team members as satisfying as possible?	❏	❏
● Given them leadership of the quality I would wish to be given myself?	❏	❏
● Noticed something new about each one's performance and development?	❏	❏
● Given each one adequate and appropriate feedback?	❏	❏
● Kept aware of everything going on in the organization that might affect me and my team?	❏	❏
● Been more confident and/or resourceful in exerting influence?	❏	❏
● Made efforts to be more productive in meetings?	❏	❏
● Improved in the ways I communicate?	❏	❏
● Given appropriate support to my manager?	❏	❏
● Obtained satisfactory support from my manager?	❏	❏
● Made sure my manager is aware of my achievements and ambitions?	❏	❏
● Done anything specific to keep up to date?	❏	❏
● Acted consistently in ways I believe to be fair and ethical?	❏	❏
● Reflected on things I have enjoyed doing and/or have done particularly well?	❏	❏

	Yes	No
• Reflected on things I have not enjoyed and/or have done less well, and considered how I might handle such things more successfully in future?	❑	❑
• Concentrated on how to improve in the future (rather than grieving about past mistakes)?	❑	❑
• Learned something about managing and/or myself as a manager?	❑	❑
• Developed my managerial competences?	❑	❑
• Worked through this checklist within the last few weeks?	❑	❑
• Additional questions to answer _____		

_____

KEY IDEA

If you have answered 'no' to any of these questions, re-read the appropriate checklists in this book – and do whatever is necessary to ensure that you do not have to give the same answer next time you give yourself your monthly check-up.